LEADERSHIP LESSONS FROM THE BIBLE

40 TIMELESS PRINCIPLES FOR 21ST CENTURY LEADERS

R. L. BRAMBLE

Leadership Lessons From The Bible
by R. L. Bramble

Printed in the United States of America

ISBN 1-59781-189-0

> P. O. Box 791104
> San Antonio, TX 78279

Scripture quotations marked KJV are taken from the *Holy Bible, The King James Version.*

Scripture quotations marked RSV are taken from the *Revised Standard Version of the Bible*, copyright 1952 [2nd edition, 1971] by the Division of Christian Education of the National Council of the Churches of Christ in the United States of America. Used by permission. All rights reserved.

Scripture quotations marked RSV, Apocrypha, are taken from the *Revised Standard Version of the Bible, Apocrypha*, copyright 1957; The third and Fourth Books of the Maccabees and Psalm 151, copyright 1977 by the Division of Christian Education of the National Council of the Churches of Christ in the United States of America. Used by permission. All rights reserved.

www.xulonpress.com

This book is dedicated to
the honor and glory of the God of the Universe,
who, in times of need,
has raised up great leaders.

ACKNOWLEDGEMENTS

There are a number of people who were instrumental in the development of this book.

First of all, I wish to thank the Christian Witness Class at Aldersgate United Methodist Church, an adult class which I have had the privilege of teaching for many years. A class discussion of "characteristics common to leaders" provided the seeds for this book. An examination of these characteristics developed into the "principles of leadership" as they are reflected in the Holy Bible.

For inspiration, I owe much to several people. The late Rev. James T. Miller, who was a true Bible scholar and worked with me on a number of Bible studies, including the Discipleship series. The Rev. Dr. David Jeremiah, Pastor of Shadow Mountain Community Church and teacher in the Turning Point Radio Ministry, who was and is a constant inspiration. The Rev. Rusty Freeman, who insisted that I become involved in all aspects of the church's leadership, and the Rev. Leighanne Brechin, who made sure that I both taught and preached.

For her continued support and encouragement, I thank my wife, Kathryn, a professional educator, who served as my critic and who helped edit the manuscript. Also, my daughters, Dr. Julia Quinlan and Kristin Koether, who were sources of encouragement for this book as well as all of my endeavors.

A special word of thanks is given to Ms. Pat Etheridge, my wife's colleague and an outstanding language arts teacher, who helped with the final editing of this book.

And last but not least, I want to thank the members of Aldersgate United Methodist Church for their continued love, support, and encouragement.

TABLE OF CONTENTS

INTRODUCTION

B efore we examine the principles which separate a leader from others, it is appropriate that we define the term "leadership."

First of all, it should be recognized that most people want to be led and that all persons are not destined to be leaders. However, at the same time, most authorities on leadership agree that leaders are made, not born. Thus, it would appear that any normal person should be able to develop his or her leadership potential and assume a leadership position under certain circumstances.

However, it is generally recognized that successful leaders practice certain principles as part of their leadership style. These principles are the main subject of this book, as we look to the Bible to provide us with examples of leaders who exemplify such principles.

One definition of leadership is as follows: *Leadership is the relationship that one person has with others, the followers, in order to attain the specific objective of the group, community, or organization.* A leader is not the result of his or her position or title—such does not make a leader. A military rank or managerial title does not in itself create a leader. Rather, it is the characteristics or principles exhibited by a leader in his or her leadership position that serves to accomplish successful achievements.

Authoritarian leaders, intoxicated by power or position, will bark orders and use intimidation in an attempt to obtain their objectives. Conversely, a good leader leads by example and earns the respect of his or her followers. Such a leader is not a pusher—he or she pulls rather than pushes. Dwight D. Eisenhower would demonstrate the art of leadership with a simple piece of string. He would put it on the table and say, "Pull it, and it will follow you anywhere you wish. Push it, and it will go nowhere at all."

Leadership is a normal and natural phenomenon which takes place within organizations. If a group of people was marooned on a desert island, after a period of time an organizational structure would emerge and a leader and perhaps sub-leaders would take charge. If an organization fails to supply the necessary leadership, the members of that organization will seek leaders, perhaps outside of the organization, for guidance. Thus, leadership is a natural process that must be fulfilled whenever human beings are brought together within an organizational setting.

These principles are exhibited in the smallest of organizations, to include the family. Paul, in several of his epistles, discusses this concept when he refers to "leadership in the home" (Ephesians 5:21-24).

As was pointed out above, anyone can hold a title or position. This, in itself, does not make that person a leader. It is the demands placed on the leader which show his or her true mettle and serve as the litmus test of leadership. This is exemplified by the old saying, "Few ships' captains prove their worth in a calm sea."

While leadership has its rewards, it is not without its problems. Leaders are often lonely and tormented as they weigh potential decisions or choices. A leader can expect to be assailed and criticized regardless of his or her achievements. But the successful leader "stays the course" and is not deterred from the determined objective by his or her critics.

What, then, is leadership? What are the principles reflected by successful leaders? It is hoped that these questions will be answered by the information provided in this book. As each principle is examined, an application of that principle is recommended so that each of us can continue to grow and mature as leaders.

Finally, we should keep in mind that leadership is not a single destination but, more importantly, a continuous journey during which we hope to grow and mature.

Let the journey continue.

1.

LEADERS ARE LIKE EAGLES, NOT LEMMINGS

But they who wait for the Lord shall renew their strength, they shall mount up with wings like eagles, they shall run and not be weary, they shall walk and not faint.
Isaiah 40:31 (RSV)

Both Saul and Jonathan slew their strongest foes, And did not return from battle empty-handed. How much they were loved, how wonderful they were—both Saul and Jonathan! They were together in life and in death. They were swifter than eagles, stronger than lions.
2 Samuel 1:22-23 (TLB)

He fills my life with good things! My youth is renewed like the eagle's! He gives justice to all who are treated fairly.
Psalm 103:5-6 (TLB)

"You have seen what I did to the Egyptians, and how I brought you to myself as though on eagle's wings."
Exodus 19:4 (TLB)

L eaders are often compared to eagles. One sign in an executive's office read, "Leaders are like eagles; they don't flock, you find them one at a time."

The eagle is a majestic bird that has been admired by human beings throughout history. It has been the subject of artists and sculptors. It has been chosen as the symbol for various nations to include the Roman Empire, Czarist Russia, Germany, and the United States. The highest leadership designation within the Boy Scouts of America is that of "Eagle Scout."

The eagle is described as a large diurnal predatory bird, with keen vision, great strength and powers of flight. Thus, it has become synonymous with strength and power. Conversely, the lemming is a small rodent, which has developed a reputation for recurrent migrations in vast numbers, often ending in its own demise by drowning.

Effective leaders are most often independent thinkers who are not easily subject to the so-called "herd-instinct," whereby someone blindly follows the rest of the group. Lemmings, however, follow each other blindly into oblivion. When one goes over the cliff, the others continue to follow until they all perish.

It is easy to succumb to the "herd-instinct." A common excuse given today is that "everyone is doing it." Therefore, it must be okay. Dictators, such as Adolph Hitler, have relied upon people responding to the lemming-like instinct of following the crowd. In a dictatorship, those who are independent thinkers and question authority or speak out in protest are eliminated.

The comparisons to the eagle in the Bible are usually in reference to God. Otherwise, they are used in comparison to the quality of strength on the part of man. It is said that young eagles are taught to fly by the bearing up of the eaglets on the wings of the adult bird. Then, while soaring, the young eaglet is allowed to try out its wings under the watchful eye of the adult. In Exodus 19:4, God tells Moses how the Hebrew people were delivered from the Egyptians in the same manner—being borne on eagle's wings.

When David was lamenting the death of Saul and Jonathan, he compared them to eagles and lions, thereby honoring their strength and accomplishments during an earlier period in their lives (see 2 Samuel 1:23).

Because of the eagle's great strength, it is often compared to a "renewal of man's strength." Of course, the source of such renewal is the Lord (See Isaiah 40:31, Hebrews 12:1-3, and Psalm 103:5).

Who are some of the leaders who deserve to be classified as "eagles?" One such leader was William Tynsdale. Determined to translate the New Testament, he fled to the Continent from England because of official opposition to his project. There he met Martin Luther and completed his New Testament . He also wrote a tract speaking out against Henry VIII's divorce. He was seized in 1535 and condemned to death while still defending his own beliefs.

Some biblical "eagles" include Noah; Joseph, son of Jacob; Moses; Gideon; Joshua; King David; and John the Baptist.

Some secular "eagles" include such leaders as George Washington, Thomas Jefferson, Nathan Hale, Abraham Lincoln, Theodore Roosevelt, and Winston Churchill.

APPLICATION: What modern leader do you consider worthy of being referred to as an "eagle?" Why? What qualities do you believe are most attributable to those leaders who should be compared to "eagles?" What qualities separate the "eagles" from the "lemmings?"

NOTES: _____

_____

_____

_____

_____

_____

_____

_____

_____

2.

LEADERS ARE
PEOPLE PERSONS

Receive her as your sister in the Lord, giving her a warm Christian welcome. Help her in every way you can, for she has helped many in their needs, including me.
Romans 16:2 (TLB)

Then representatives of all the tribes of Israel came to David at Hebron and gave him their pledge of loyalty. "We are your blood brothers," they said. "And even when Saul was our king you were our real leader. The Lord has said that you should be shepherd and leader of his people."
2 Samuel 5:1-2 (TLB)

The ultimate criterion for becoming a leader is that he or she has followers. Without followers, no one can be a leader regardless of what title or rank he or she holds. Thus, since leaders must have followers, effective leaders must be "people persons."

In organizations, there are two types of positions of responsibility: line and staff. The line positions make up the leadership positions within the organization while the staff positions are responsible for providing support to the line positions.

Perhaps the military is the best example of line and staff

relationships. The line officers, commissioned and non-commissioned, are responsible for leading the troops. The staff positions provide information and support to the line officers. In fact, the United States Army has created a position in response to this situation known as the "specialist." A specialist fourth class (E-4) is the same pay grade as a corporal while a specialist fifth class is the same pay grade as a sergeant (E-5). However, the corporal and sergeant have line authority while the specialists do not.

Thus, a staff person may have subordinates and not be considered a leader. Such subordinates are necessary to complete the staff function's responsibilities. Typical staff functions within organizations include such support areas as accounting, personnel, and research and development, among others.

To be a "people person," a leader must not only have followers but must genuinely like people. He or she must like being with people, being responsible for people, and being their leader. A person who doesn't like people should not be in a leadership position but, rather, should seek a staff position where he or she can function alone or with minimal contact with others.

Phoebe was a leader who liked people and who helped many (Romans 16:2). Paul recognized her ability and it is believed that he entrusted her with the delivery of his letter to the church in Rome. Paul, himself, was a "people person." In Romans 16:3-15, Paul lists numerous people who were to be greeted in Rome—people Paul knew—even though at the time of the writing of this letter he had never been to Rome. Like most preachers and evangelists, Paul was a "people person."

King David was obviously a "people person." The Scriptures indicate that David enjoyed being in the company of others and that he liked to sing (2 Samuel 22:1) and dance (2 Samuel 6:14). He could attract followers as only a "people person" can.

When considering candidates for leadership positions, an important factor is a determination of the candidate's "people skills." No one wants to be led by an arrogant bully who has little regard for his or her followers. The successful leader understands the "human side" of management and knows that "followship" must be earned. Moreover, such a leader often begins by identifying with his or her followers in order to determine exactly what is required to attract followers in the first place. Like that old saying, "You can't fool dogs or babies," a leader who is not a "people person" won't be able to fool his or her followers for long.

Leaders who possess effective people skills interact with their followers in a positive way that includes: treating them with respect, motivating them, teaching and mentoring them, allowing them to grow, and maintaining effective and open lines of communication.

Successful leaders know that it is the people who make up organizations. For example, it has been said that an airline is five percent metal and 95 percent people. Likewise, a church is primarily people, rather than bricks and mortar. Therefore, the effective leaders of such organizations must be "people persons."

Andrew Carnegie, the great industrialist, recognized the importance of his people when he declared that, if he were stripped of all his material wealth but retained the people in his organization, he could rebuild his business in four years.

APPLICATION: Do you consider yourself a "people person?" Can you name an effective modern leader who is not a "people person?" What can you do to develop your people skills to a higher level?

NOTES: _____

_____

_____

_____

_____

_____

_____

_____

_____

Reflections on Your Leadership Journey

In the space below, record your reflections or thoughts
as you continue your leadership journey:

3.

LEADERS HAVE ADMINISTRATIVE SKILLS

❖⟨▬▭⟩◗⟨▬▭⟩◗❖

Turning to Joseph, Pharaoh said to him, "...I am hereby appointing you to be in charge of this entire project. What you say goes, throughout all the land of Egypt. I alone will outrank you."

Genesis 41:39-40 (TLB)

If God has given you administrative ability and put you in charge of the work of others, take the responsibility seriously.

Romans 12:8b (TLB)

A prudent man foresees the difficulties ahead and prepares for them; the simpleton goes blindly on and suffers the consequences.

Proverbs 22:3 (TLB)

Any enterprise is built by wise planning, becomes strong through common sense, and profits wonderfully by keeping abreast of the facts.

Proverbs 24:3-4 (TLB)

Effective leaders must possess administrative skills. Leadership is but one function—albeit perhaps the most important function—of the management process.

Thus, leaders are also administrators or managers. They are responsible for assuring that the work gets done. Joseph was such an administrator. He was second only to the Pharaoh and was responsible for managing the kingdom and planning for the predicted famine.

It has been said that "management is a process"—a unique process that is made up of several fundamental activities which are referred to as *Planning, Organizing, Leading,* and *Controlling.* The functions are universal and are applicable to the work of any administrator, such as a college dean, a sales manager, a hospital administrator, a church pastor, or a military commander. Each of these management functions is summarized as follows:

- *Planning* – To determine the objectives and a course of action to be taken.
- *Organizing* – To distribute the work among the group and to establish lines of authority and responsibility.
- *Leading* – To move the people to action and to assure that the group carries out their prescribed tasks effectively and enthusiastically.
- *Controlling* – To continually take corrective action in order to assure that the actual performance conforms with the prior planning.

While in graduate school, one of the author's professors presented the functions of management (administration) succinctly in the schematic which is shown below.[1] The functions shown are: *Plan, Organize, Lead,* and *Control.* The resources, which the manager has at his or her disposal, are: *people, money, time, materials* (including equipment), and *space* (facilities). The leader's proper utilization of these resources will be instrumental in determining his or her ability to function as an administrator.

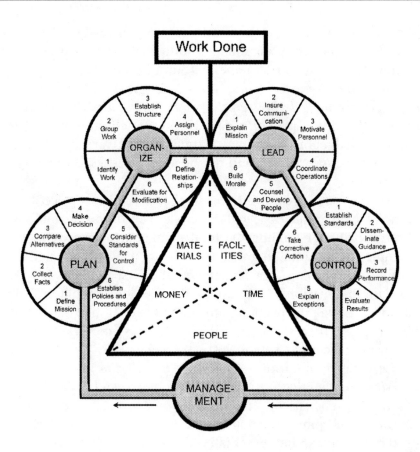

Although it can and should be argued that "leading" takes place during all four functions, Dr. Stephenson has depicted them as occurring separately in four distinctly separate functions. In the paragraphs which follow, we will briefly examine each of the four functions of management.

Planning is generally considered to be the first function since successful organizations rarely exist unless effective planning has occurred. Thus, good planning is necessary to the successful achievement of the organization. Six elements are shown in the planning process: d*efine mission, collect facts, compare alternatives, make a decision, consider standards for control,* and *establish policies and procedures.*

Organization, or *Organizing*, is discussed in greater detail as a "principle" in a subsequent chapter. Organizing, as seen in the above schematic, serves to develop the organizational structure and the assignment of personnel within each level of the organization. The six specific elements found in the organizing function are: i*dentify work, group the work, establish the structure, assign personnel, define relationships,* and *evaluate for modification.* Without a proper organization, which includes trained and knowledgeable personnel assigned to the various organizational levels, the "work" will not be accomplished efficiently or effectively.

As was stated previously, "leading" actually takes place during each of the other functions and should not be isolated except for the purpose of understanding the total management process. As an example, in the planning function the first element listed was "define the mission." In leadership, the first element listed is "explain the mission." "Explaining the mission" should probably take place during the planning process or not later than the organizing process. To borrow an old cliché, it is important that all members of the organization "be on the same page."

Leading, in addition to *defining the mission*, also includes: i*nsuring communications, motivating personnel, coordinating operations, counseling and developing people,* and *building morale.* Good communications, likewise, must be present during all of the functions, but especially during the "organizing" and "controlling" aspects of the management process. Poor communications is a common cause of failure within organizations. Part of communicating includes coordinating operations so that everyone has a clear understanding of the goals and objectives. The leader is responsible for counseling and developing those people immediately subordinate to him or her. Moreover, good morale is imperative if the organization is going to attract and keep good workers (this includes volunteer workers within a non-profit organizational structure).

The ***Controlling*** function is required to assure that the "planning" remains on-track. Such can be compared to determining a ship's destination. The captain of a ship charts a course and, working through his navigator, assures that corrective action is constantly taken to keep the ship on its charted course. If a hurricane is in the path of the ship, the leader must chart a new course, but one which will ultimately allow the ship to reach its original destination. Moreover, sometimes the corrective action involves additional planning, i.e., "going back to the drawing board."

The six elements shown in the above schematic for the "controlling" function are: e*stablish standards, disseminate guidance, record performance, explain exceptions,* and *take corrective action.* An example of the controlling function can be applied to a church budget, but is applicable to a business organization as well. The church develops a budget as part of the planning process. The standards for control are those methods that will be used to determine the effectiveness of the budget. At each level of the organization, the leader, who is responsible for his or her part of the budget, is given this information and instructed in what he or she can or cannot do ("disseminate guidance"). As the funds are received through tithes and gifts each month and then are spent, such is recorded and provided to the responsible leaders ("recording performance"). This information is continually evaluated and compared to the original budget (the "plan"). Exceptions are explained, i.e., "We didn't receive what was expected in total giving because attendance was down." Or, "The disaster of 911 has resulted in an overall decline in giving."

Thus, "corrective action" is what the leader/administrator takes when the results are different from the "plan." With a budget, it may mean reducing the projected spending if the funds do not equal the amount projected. Or, perhaps it will require that the church have a "fund raising" activity in order to produce additional income. Such corrective action involves "new planning" and "new organizing," which will be followed by "additional controlling." All of these revised functions will be implemented under the management function of "leading."

Although not specifically listed, "research and development" within organizations involves both the "planning" and "controlling" functions. John Erick Jonsson, the former head of Texas Instruments and a former Mayor of Dallas, has defined research and development (also referred to as R & D) in the following way: *"[It is] what you had better have been doing before you find out that you can't continue doing what you're doing now."* Such R & D includes the constant monitoring of those forces of change which continue to affect the organization and its defined mission.

In this chapter we have only touched briefly on the administrative skills required by leaders. In one university textbook on the *Principles of Management*, some 520 pages have been devoted to the four functions of "planning, organizing, leading, and controlling."

Joseph was given the responsibility to prepare the people of Egypt for a famine. He had seven plentiful years to make sure that sufficient grain was stored to feed the people during the subsequent seven years of famine. Joseph was an effective and efficient administrator and surely used all of the functions discussed in this chapter to accomplish the "defined mission."

APPLICATION: What kind of administrator are you? How is an administrator different from a leader? Or, is there any difference? How will you implement the functions of Planning, Organizing, and Controlling, along with leadership skills, in your organization?

NOTES: _____

_____
_____
_____
_____
_____
_____
_____
_____

4.

LEADERS PRACTICE ORGANIZATIONAL SKILLS

-+>═◐ ◑═+-

...Moses sat as usual to hear the people's complaints against each other, from morning to evening. When Moses' father-in-law saw how much time he was taking, he said, "Why are you trying to do all this alone, with the people standing here all day long to get your help...It's not right...Now listen, and let me give you a word of advice and God will bless you.... Find some capable, godly, honest men who hate bribes, and appoint them as judges, one judge for each 1,000 people; he in turn will have ten judges under him, each in charge of a hundred; and under each of them will be two judges, each responsible for the affairs of fifty people; and each of these will have five judges beneath him, each counseling ten persons. Let these men be responsible to serve the people with justice at all times. Anything that is too important or complicated can be brought to you...." Moses listened to his father-in-law's advice, and followed this suggestion.

Exodus 18:13; 17-20a; 21-24 (TLB)

Moses' father-in-law, Jethro, may have been the first management consultant in recorded history. He recognized that

Moses could not effectively handle all of the problems of the entire population of the Children of Israel who had been brought out of slavery in Egypt. As Exodus 18 points out, Moses was trying to do it all—and the result was "disorganization."

Jethro's advice was to organize and to implement what is recognized as an organizational structure, one that is used today by the military, business organizations, non-profit organizations, and even the church. Such an organizational structure, which is often represented by an "organization chart," utilizes the management principles of "delegation of authority" and "span of control."

The following illustration reflects what Moses was trying to do during the period prior to Jethro's advice, resulting in **"disorganization."** [2]

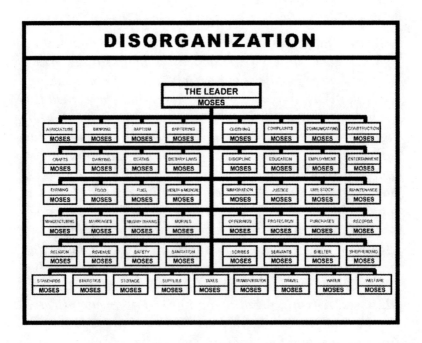

The second illustration reflects the result of Jethro's advice, which was **"organization."** [3]

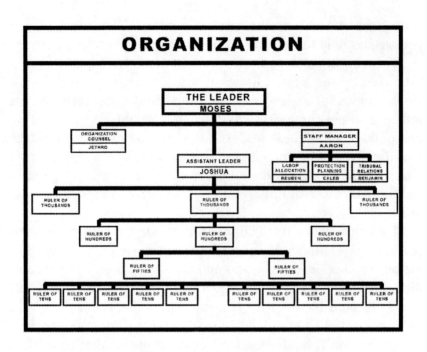

A common mistake made by some leaders is to think that no one can do a particular job better than he or she can. Thus, the leader tries to do everything by himself or herself. Effective leaders must learn to delegate when they are in charge of more work than they can personally accomplish alone. Andrew Carnegie, the great industrialist, was a strong advocate of delegation of authority. He has been quoted as saying, "When a man realizes he can call others in to help him do a job better than he can do it alone, he has taken a big step in his life."

Likewise, the management principle of "span of control" is applicable in organizational structures and must be utilized in conjunction with the principle of delegation of authority. Span of control is concerned with the number of persons that any one leader can effectively supervise at any one time. The organizational structure, which Jethro described to Moses, applies this principle: *with no one "judge" or leader having to supervise more than ten people.*

While a chief executive officer of a large organization of 10,000 people may be seen as "being in charge" of everyone, he or she, in fact, has only five or ten people who report directly to him or her.

This is the effective use of "span of control." Then, each of those persons has only ten or fewer people reporting to each of them.

This concept of organization is seen in the organizational structure used by the United States Army. The army has established various ranks for its leaders, consisting of generals, colonels, lieutenant colonels, majors, captains, lieutenants, sergeants, and corporals. Each of these leaders has a specific responsibility and a specific number of immediate subordinates. These leaders are in charge of divisions, battle groups, battalions, companies, platoons, and squads, all with only ten to twelve persons reporting to any one leader.

The organizational structure recommended by Jethro also incorporates the leadership principle of "exception." That is, those matters too important or too complicated to be decided by a subordinate can be referred to the higher authority—the one who is ultimately responsible for what happens within that particular level of the organization. Thus, delegation of authority does not mean that the leader can "pass the buck." Rather, it means that he or she is ultimately responsible for everything that happens within a particular level of the organization, i.e., he or she has only delegated, not relinquished, the responsibility that extends to the lowest level. The ultimate responsibility remains with the leader. President Harry S. Truman recognized this principle when he placed a sign in the Oval Office which stated, "The Buck Stops Here."

Effective church organizations utilize this same concept of organizational structure. Large congregations could not function effectively without it. There is usually a senior pastor, one or more associate pastors, one or more administrators, a board chairperson, a board of trustees or administrative council, and numerous committees, each of which has a chairperson. Without such a structure, the result would be an ineffective and chaotic organization that would accomplish little.

However, a word of caution is in order. A leader must take great care in selecting those persons who will serve in key positions within the organization. Jethro pointed this out to Moses when he said, "Find some capable, godly, honest men who hate bribes..." Thus, the first rule of delegation is that the person selected to handle a particular position of responsibility must be capable of actually performing in the assigned position.

An important secondary benefit of delegation is that a leader has the opportunity to develop subordinates as they learn to handle the particular responsibilities assigned to them. Thus, each leader is responsible for mentoring, encouraging, and developing subordinates at each level within the organization. This is in keeping with an important standard which is common within many organizations: "You can't be promoted until you have developed and trained someone to take over your current responsibility."

"Responsibility" has been defined as *the obligation of an individual to carry out assigned activities to the best of his or her ability.* Such responsibility comes into existence because a person with authority delegates such authority for the performance of a specific task, function, or objective.

Like Moses, we must learn to choose capable individuals and delegate to them the responsibility and authority necessary to accomplish the objectives or mission of our organization.

APPLICATION: Do you understand the importance of delegation of authority and span of control? Do you use these principles in your own organization? Can you remember seeing the improper use of these principles within an organization? What actions will you take to ensure that your organization utilizes these principles effectively?

NOTES: _____

_____

_____

_____

_____

_____

_____

_____

Reflections on Your Leadership Journey

In the space below, record your reflections or thoughts
as you continue your leadership journey:

5.

LEADERS PUT THEIR FOLLOWERS FIRST

◆➤═◉═◀◆

I wrote to the church, but Diotrephes, who loves to be first, will have nothing to do with us. So if I come, I will call attention to what he is doing, gossiping maliciously about us. Not satisfied with that, he refuses to welcome the brothers. He also stops those who want to do so and puts them out of the church.

3 John 9-10 (NIV)

So Moses went back to the Lord and said, "Oh, what a great sin these people have committed! They have made themselves gods of gold. But now, please forgive their sin—but if not, then blot me out of the book you have written." The Lord replied to Moses, "Whoever has sinned against me I will blot out of my book. Now go, lead the people to the place I spoke of...."

Exodus 32:31-34a (NIV)

Effective leaders put the needs of their followers first. Such leaders are concerned sincerely with the welfare of their people. In the military, a commander is to make sure that his or her troops are taken care of first. For example, only after the men have been fed is the commander to eat.

Unfortunately, this principle is not practiced in most organizations including the church. Many leaders put themselves first and practice the philosophy of "looking out for number one." Such was the case of Diotrephes. It appears that Diotrephes was the leader of a congregation in Corinth and who rejected both John and certain ones of his followers. As John wrote, "Diotrephes...loves to be first."

In sharp contrast, Moses was willing to plead for the forgiveness of the sinful Hebrew people whom he had led out of slavery in Egypt. Moses was willing to have God "blot him out of His book" in exchange for God's sparing of the errant people whom Moses was responsible for leading. While God responded that He would hold the people responsible for their own sins, Moses was to continue to lead the people in their journey to the Promised Land.

In most organizations today, employees are expected to be loyal to their employer and its leaders. Effective leaders must remember that loyalty is a "two-way street." Leaders, who expect loyalty from their followers, must show through their own actions that their followers' welfare is a major subject of their concern.

All of us have known a leader who always blames others, including subordinates, so that he or she can look good. Such leaders only care about themselves and not their followers. They are unwilling to give priority to the welfare of those under their leadership. Such leaders seldom earn the respect of their subordinates and eventually are found out by their own superiors.

Effective leaders don't put themselves first. Rather, the needs of the group are considered paramount. General George S. Patton, one of the most successful military leaders in terms of getting the job done, was reported as saying:

> *A general officer, who will invariably assume the responsibility for failure, whether he deserves it or not, and invariably give the credit for success to others, whether they deserve it or not, will achieve outstanding success.*[4]

Patton, although often criticized by people outside of his command as being "hungry for glory," was always eager to credit those under his command for all that he had accomplished. Patton was known to continually issue commendations and bestow praise on the members of his command. He didn't use "I" but, rather, used "we," which is the mark of a successful leader.

A *boss* says, "I," while a leader says, "we." A *boss* fixes blame, while a leader solves problems and fixes mistakes.

APPLICATION: What leaders have you observed who put their people first? How do you feel about a leader who takes all the credit but never any of the blame? How can you become a leader who puts your followers first?

NOTES: _____

_____

_____

_____

_____

_____

_____

_____

_____

Reflections on Your Leadership Journey

In the space below, record your reflections or thoughts
as you continue your leadership journey:

6.

LEADERS MENTOR AND ENCOURAGE OTHERS

⋄⇥════⊃ ⊂════⇤⋄

Barnabas was a kindly person, full of the Holy Spirit and strong in faith. As a result, large numbers of people were added to the Lord. Then Barnabas went on to Tarsus to hunt for Paul. When he found him, he brought him back to Antioch; and both of them stayed there for a full year, teaching the many new converts. (It was there in Antioch that the believers were first called "Christians.")

Acts 11:24-26 (TLB)

A leader has a responsibility for developing other aspiring leaders, often when they are his or her subordinates. A successful leader does not feel threatened by other aspiring leaders who exhibit talents and abilities, which, in some cases, may allow a younger, less experienced person to surpass the teacher or mentor.

Such was the case with Barnabas and Paul. Paul's veracity and sincerity were subject to question by the early church leaders in Jerusalem to include the apostles Peter and James, the brother of Jesus. Such an attitude on the part of the leaders of the early church is understandable in light of Paul's prior persecution of the fledgling

Christian church.

Perhaps Paul doubted that he had a role as a leader in the early church, even though he had been commissioned by the Lord, Himself, on the road to Damascus. Apparently discouraged, Paul had returned to Tarsus where he remained for some 10 years.

Barnabas saw in Paul the potential of leadership. Barnabas traveled to Tarsus and brought Paul to Antioch, where Barnabas was the leader of the local church. Later, Barnabas spoke as an advocate on Paul's behalf before the church fathers in Jerusalem. After convincing the leaders of the early church to give Paul a chance, Barnabas took Paul with him on his first missionary journey to preach the Gospel to the Gentiles.

Beginning in the 11th chapter of Acts, the two men are referred to as "Barnabas and Paul." However, following Acts 13:43, the Scriptures refer to them as "Paul and Barnabas" as Paul assumed the greater leadership role.

Thus, because of Barnabas' encouragement and mentoring of Paul, coupled with the grace of God, a great leader emerged in the Christian church—a leader who brought the message of Jesus Christ to the Gentile world and who is personally responsible for writing the majority of the books in the New Testament.

It is interesting to note that the name "Barnabas" means "Son of Encouragement," although his given name was actually Joseph.

Frequently, an aspiring leader needs only to be given a chance by one who has faith and confidence in his or her ability. Such was the case with President Abraham Lincoln and Ulysses S. Grant. Although Grant had failed previously in his various endeavors and had resigned his commission at the request of his previous military commander, Lincoln saw in him the potential of a great military leader. Grant was chosen by the President to lead the Union Army over the criticism and resistance of others. General Grant proved that President Lincoln had made a good choice as he led the Union Army to numerous victories, which culminated in the surrender of the Confederacy by General Robert E. Lee in 1865. Three years later, in 1868, Ulysses S. Grant was elevated to the highest leadership position in this country when he was elected President of the United States.

APPLICATION: Are you mentoring and encouraging someone to become a leader? Who do you know who has the potential for successful leadership and who needs only the encouragement and support of someone who believes in him or her?

NOTES: _____

_____

_____

_____

_____

_____

_____

_____

_____

_____

Reflections on Your Leadership Journey

In the space below, record your reflections or thoughts
as you continue your leadership journey:

7.

LEADERS ARE AWARE OF THE CHARISMA FACTOR

⋅✦⟹◉⟸✦⋅

Now no one in Israel was such a handsome specimen of manhood as Absalom, and no one else received such praise... And when anyone came to bow to him Absalom wouldn't let him, but shook his hand instead! So in this way Absalom stole the hearts of all the people of Israel.... A messenger soon arrived in Jerusalem to tell King David, "All Israel has joined Absalom in a conspiracy against you!"

2 Samuel 14:25; 15:6, 13 (TLB)

As it happened, a Jew named Apollos, a wonderful Bible teacher and preacher, had just arrived in Ephesus from Alexandria in Egypt.

Acts 18:24 (TLB)

But, dear brothers, I beg you in the name of the Lord Jesus Christ to stop arguing among yourselves. Let there be real harmony so that there won't be splits in the Church... Some of you are saying, "I am a follower of Paul"; and others say that they are for Apollos or for Peter; and some that they alone are the true followers of Christ.

1 Corinthians 1:10a, 12 (TLB)

Charisma has been described as an extraordinary power in a person that serves to win the support of others. Charisma is a quality that enables a leader to attract followers.

While charisma is not a quality that one must have to be a leader, it is a quality that enables many leaders to garner followers quickly and easily. Unfortunately, some leaders, who may have charisma, lack a depth of character and, ultimately, prove to be bad leaders who are nothing more than "wolves in sheep's clothing."

Absalom, King David's third son, was such a person. He was attractive in appearance, charming in manners, and popular with the people. However, he secretly plotted to take the kingship from his father, David, by force. He took advantage of this natural appeal and his handsome appearance to win the favor of the people. When David learned of Absalom's rebellious acts, he had to flee (2 Samuel 17:24) and Absalom was formally anointed as king after taking control of Jerusalem (2 Samuel 19:10).

Apollos was an eloquent Jew and quickly became an influential leader in the early church. However, his knowledge was limited since he knew only the baptism of John (Acts 18:25) and only some of the teachings of Jesus. But, he was apparently quite popular and contributed to a division in the church at Corinth when the people became divided over whom they should follow.

In this modern day of television, people are drawn to those who are handsome and eloquent. John F. Kennedy had this type of appeal, which was certainly a factor in his becoming elected as President. When the Kennedy-Nixon debates were held, those who watched the debates on television said that Kennedy had won, while those who heard the debates on the radio thought that Nixon had won. Kennedy was able to project charisma though his handsome appearance, keen wit, and flashing smile. Conversely, television viewers saw a Nixon who appeared "sweaty" with a "five o'clock shadow." John F. Kennedy had charisma.

Would Abraham Lincoln have been elected if television had existed when he and Stephen A. Douglas debated? What role did charisma have in the elections of Ronald Reagan and Bill Clinton?

Adolph Hitler was an eloquent speaker who could hold his

audience spell-bound for hours. Fidel Castro has shown a similar charisma. However, history has proved that both were lacking in the standard of character which leaders should possess.

On January 17, 1998, President Clinton gave a deposition in the Paula Jones' sexual harassment suit against him. During nearly six hours of testimony, he denied having had a sexual relationship with former White House intern Monica Lewinsky. Clinton's popularity continues today even though he subsequently admitted that he did, in fact, have a sexual relationship with Lewinsky. Is such continued popularity the result of charisma?

Charisma alone is not enough. The effective leader must be a person of substance—a person who has the depth of character necessary to properly lead his or her followers toward a realistic and proper goal.

Thus, the effective leader should be aware of the "charisma factor." Such awareness allows him or her to see through the superficial veneer of those who lead out of pure popularity or charismatic appeal.

APPLICATION: What do you think should be the role of charisma in selecting leaders? Name two or more modern leaders who you believe exemplify charisma. Do you think that you have charisma?

NOTES: _____

_____
_____
_____
_____
_____
_____
_____
_____

Reflections on Your Leadership Journey

In the space below, record your reflections or thoughts
as you continue your leadership journey:

8.

LEADERS EXPECT
AND ACCEPT CRITICISM

Now they left Elim and journeyed on into the Sihn Wilderness, between Elim and Mt. Sinai, arriving there on the fifteenth day of the second month after leaving Egypt. There, too, the people spoke bitterly against Moses and Aaron. "Oh, that we were back in Egypt," they moaned, "and that the Lord had killed us there! For there we had plenty to eat. But now you have brought us into this wilderness to kill us with starvation."

Exodus 16:1-3 (TLB)

Don't refuse to accept criticism; get all the help you can.

Proverbs 23:12 (TLB)

The only way for a leader not to be criticized is to do nothing. However, that is not totally true either, for the leader who does nothing may well be criticized for doing nothing.

A leader can expect criticism. It comes with the territory. There are numerous examples from the Bible of leaders who were criticized for their actions. And some deserved to be criticized.

As Moses attempted to lead the Children of Israel through the wilderness as God had directed him to do, he was criticized along the way. The people continually complained about their living conditions, not having enough to eat, and things in general. The above Scripture reference is but one example. But Moses was their leader and he took their criticism in stride.

Even when God wanted to destroy them following the incident with the golden calf (see Exodus 32:7-11), Moses pled their case as their leader and protector. And, God granted Moses' petition and spared the errant Hebrew children.

Leaders are often lonely. And criticism becomes part of the territory of the leader. Almost everyone praises the leader when things are going well for the followers. But, when the going gets tough, the criticism begins. And, if a leader slips and falls, that is often the one thing we most remember about him or her.

Thus, the leader needs to expect criticism and to gain strength from it. Theodore Roosevelt was criticized, especially in later years when he again ran for President of the United States on an independent party ticket (his first term as President was as a Republican). As a result of such criticism, he penned the following, which has served as a credo of many modern leaders:

> *It's not the critic who counts, not the man who points out how the strong man stumbled, or where the doer of deeds could have done them better. The credit belongs to the man who is actually in the arena; whose face is marred by the dust and sweat and blood; who strives valiantly; who errs and comes short again and again...who knows the great enthusiasms, the great devotions and spends himself in a worthy cause; who, at best, knows in the end the triumph of high achievement and who, at worst, if he fails, at least fails while daring greatly so that his place shall never be with those cold and timid souls who knew neither victory nor defeat.*

Leaders do not always win or achieve the specific goal sought. Every battle does not result in a victory. Defeats and set backs are to be expected. How a leader handles his or her setbacks and defeats often determines the true mettle of the leader. And a true leader often gains strength from the small defeats in order to go on to achieve greatness. Moses did lead the children of Israel out of slavery and to the Jordan River. There he passed the mantle of leadership to Joshua, and the Israelites entered the Promised Land.

APPLICATION: It's not the critic who counts! The leader must be able to accept criticism, both constructive and destructive, and continue to work toward the determined goal. How will you handle criticism?

NOTES: _____

_____

_____

_____

_____

_____

_____

_____

_____

_____

Reflections on Your Leadership Journey

In the space below, record your reflections or thoughts
as you continue your leadership journey:

9.

LEADERS REFUSE TO QUIT

--*≡◯≡*--

About that time King Herod moved against some of the believers, and killed the apostle James (John's brother). When Herod saw how much this pleased the Jewish leaders, he arrested Peter during the Passover celebration and imprisoned him, placing him under the guard of sixteen soldiers. Herod's intention was to deliver Peter to the Jews for execution after the Passover.

Acts 12:1-4 (TLB)

A mob was quickly formed against Paul and Silas and the judges ordered them stripped and beaten with wooden whips. Again and again the rods slashed down across their bare backs; and afterwards they were thrown into prison. The jailer was threatened with death if they escaped, so he took no chances, but put them into the inner dungeon and clamped their feet into the stocks.

Acts 16:22-24 (TLB)

Members of the United States Marines pride themselves in the fact that they "never retreat." However, upon occasion, they have found it necessary to "advance to the rear." A leader's refusal to quit is a mind-set—it becomes a mental attitude.

Nelson Mandela, as a lawyer and a leader of the black people in South Africa, refused to give up his fight against the rule of apartheid in South Africa. As a result, he was imprisoned for some 27 years. During his imprisonment, Mandela was offered the opportunity on more than one occasion to be released from prison—a release conditional on his agreement to leave South Africa and no longer speak out against the practice of apartheid. Nelson Mandela remained in prison as a continuing symbol to the black people of South Africa and to the rest of the world of his refusal to quit a cause for which he had dedicated himself.

The early church leaders, to include Peter, Paul and Silas, refused to quit preaching the gospel and recruiting new believers even though they were beaten and imprisoned. They would not quit.

The English lay preacher, John Bunyan, served some 12 years in prison for preaching without a license. He could have been released from prison if he had agreed to refrain from his preaching. He refused to do so. During this time in prison, he began writing *The Pilgrim's Progress* (published in 1678), a great literary work, which remains widely read today.

During World War II, Winston Churchill, as the elected leader of the British Empire, rallied his people to never quit. During one of his more famous speeches, he challenged England's embattled citizens with these words:

> *We shall go on to the end, we shall fight in France, we shall fight on the seas and oceans, we shall defend our island, whatever the cost may be; we shall fight on the beaches, we shall fight on the landing grounds, we shall fight in the fields and in the streets, we shall fight in the hills; we shall never surrender.*

Some years following the end of World War II, Churchill was asked to give the commencement address at a school graduation. Everyone waited in anticipation to hear this great orator, a recipient of the Nobel Prize for Literature. After a lengthy introduction befitting a former Prime Minister of Great Britain, Churchill assumed his position on the rostrum. He said, "Never, never, never, never give up!" He then promptly sat down. These few words, uttered by this great world leader, spoke volumes.

George Gershwin composed almost 100 melodies before he sold his first one for which he received $5. During his first five years as a writer, Zane Grey couldn't sell a single story. Gershwin and Grey refused to quit.

The inventor, Thomas Edison, took some 3,000 attempts before he discovered the correct filaments for the lightbulb—but he refused to quit. Walt Disney ultimately built a billon dollar empire consisting of motion picture studios, cartoon characters, and theme parks. However, early in his career, he was fired by a newspaper for lacking ideas and later had to file for bankruptcy. Walt Disney refused to quit.

When leaders know in their hearts they are right, they should refuse to quit. As Paul wrote in his letter to the Philippians, "I can do all things through Christ who strengthens me" (Philippians 4:13).

The following poem is one which leaders should read anytime they are considering giving up on a worthwhile cause:

> *If you think you are beaten, you are.*
> *If you think you dare not, you don't.*
> *If you like to win but think you can't,*
> *It's almost certain that you won't.*
> *Life's battles don't always go*
> *To the stronger woman or man,*
> *But sooner or later, those who win*
> *Are those who think they can.*
> *(Author unknown)*

The leader, who refuses to quit and continues to pursue a worthy cause to the end, should be able to say, like the apostle Paul, "I have fought the good fight, I have finished the race, I have kept the faith" (2 Timothy 4:7).

APPLICATION: When have you wanted to quit when you knew in your heart you should continue? When have you actually quit when you could have continued? What will prevent you from quitting in the future?

NOTES: _____

_____

_____

_____

_____

_____

_____

_____

_____

10.

LEADERS EMBRACE THE INEVITABILITY OF CHANGE

⤟⇒⇐⤞

Just after daybreak, Jesus stood on the beach; but the disciples did not know it was Jesus. Jesus said to them, "Children, you have no fish, have you?" They answered him, " No." He said to them, "Cast the net to the right side of the boat, and you will find some." So they cast it, and now they were not able to haul it in because there were so many fish. …So Simon Peter went aboard and hauled the net ashore, full of large fish, a hundred and fifty-three of them; and though there were many, the net was not torn.
John 21:4-6;11 (NRSV)

While Peter was still speaking, the Holy Spirit fell upon all who heard the word. The circumcised believers who had come with Peter were astounded that the gift of the Holy Spirit had been poured out even on the Gentiles.
Acts 10:44-45 (NRSV)

It is human nature to be resistant to change. However, as leaders, we should be constantly reminded of the old maxim: "The only thing that remains constant in the world is change itself."

Peter and the early leaders of the church saw Christianity as a sect of the Jewish faith, one that did not include the Gentiles. A review of the Scriptures, both the Old Testament and the New Testament teachings of Jesus, clearly reveal that the message of God was not limited to the Jews. However, Peter and the early church leaders were resistant to any change that would include the "uncircumcised" Gentiles.

We, too, are resistant to change, even when the change is for the better. We, too, easily fall into that rut of saying, "We've always done it that way."

It has been reported that in the late 1800s there was a serious discussion about closing the United States Patent Office because anything that would be invented had been invented. Following World War II, it was thought that 12 large-scale computers would be all this nation would ever need. During the 1980s, a computer with 100 megabytes of memory was thought to be sufficient for almost any application. Today, personal computers can be purchased with 40 or more gigabytes.

Major changes are seen almost everywhere. Pay telephones have become almost obsolete because most of us own cell phones. The changes in medical science continue to amaze even the most erudite among us. Other technological changes during the 20th century are too numerous to list but, include such innovations as: the jet plane; modern automobiles; color television; space travel; the internet, with all of the possibilities of e-commerce; and satellite communications, just to name a few.

The story has been circulated that Fred Smith, the founder of Federal Express, created the concept of "hub and spokes logistics" and submitted an academic paper to his university professor outlining the concept of FedEx. While his paper was not rejected, he was not without a number of skeptics who viewed the concept as a radical change that was not feasible. Mr. Smith went on to create Federal Express (now known as FedEx®) in 1971—a company which continues to operate successfully throughout the world.

In 1905, the University of Bern turned down the Ph.D. dissertation of a young physics student as being fanciful and irrelevant. The professors were not willing to consider the changes represented by these ideas. However, Albert Einstein, who is now considered to be one of the greatest minds of the 20th century, went on to develop such ideas into what became widely accepted theories.

In 1803, the British posted a military detachment on the cliffs of Dover to watch for Napoleon. Napoleon died in 1821. However, in 1927 the guard unit was still assigned to the cliffs of Dover because there had always been a guard unit posted there.

Perhaps one of the best examples "of resistance to change" is the following story, which occurred when Bismarck was Prussian Ambassador to the court of Alexander II in the early 1860s:

> *Bismarck looked out a window of the Peterhof Palace and saw a sentry on duty in the middle of the lawn. He asked the Czar why the man was there. The Czar asked the aide-de-camp, who did not know.*
>
> *He sent for the officer in command, who did not know, either.*
>
> *The general commanding the troops at Peterhof was summoned. The Czar barked, "General, why is that soldier stationed in that isolated place?" The General replied, "It is in accordance with the ancient custom."*
>
> *The Czar then demanded to know the origin of the ancient custom. The General replied, "I do not recollect." To which the Czar demanded a full investigation and report.*
>
> *After three days, it was reported that the sentry was posted by an order put on the books some 80 years before. It appeared that, one morning in the spring of 1780, Catherine the Great had looked out on that lawn and seen the first flower of spring thrusting its head above the previously frozen soil. She ordered a sentry to be posted to prevent anyone from picking the flower.*
>
> *And in 1860 there was still a sentry on the lawn—a memorial to habit, custom, or just because "We've always done it that way."*

Organizations that are resistant to change and refuse to adapt to new developments in the market place may soon be left behind. Xerox Corporation's Palo Alto, California, engineers and scientists invented both the personal computer and the "mouse." But its managers in Connecticut preferred to concentrate solely on copiers and allowed other companies, such as Apple Computer, to end up with these products. With an attitude that was resistant to change, Xerox lost a large market share to the far-sighted Japanese copier companies, such as Canon and Sharp (Xerox nearly went out of business in the late 1970s). Sears Roebuck, once the world's largest retailer, saw Wal-Mart replace it as number one. And Sears' former retailing rival, Montgomery Ward, no longer exists.

Peter and the other disciples, who were described in the 21st chapter of John, were experienced fishermen. Yet they caught no fish until Jesus told them to fish on the other side of the boat. They were required to make a change. And the number of fish they caught—153—is representative of all of the species of fish known to exist. Thus, symbolically, Peter and the disciples, who had been instructed previously to become "fishers of men" (Matthew 4:19 RSV), were taught that the Gospel is applicable to all of mankind, not just to the Jews. This required a major change in their thinking. It was a paradigm shift.

A prominent church leader and pastor was recently quoted as saying, "Any church that's not changing is dying." This statement is applicable to all organizations, both sectarian and secular. The direction and change within an organization rests upon its leaders. It is the leaders who must implement the change.

Thus, change is inevitable. To resist change is to invite disappointment and defeat. When leaders accept change, and use it to their advantage, it becomes an ally rather than an adversary.

APPLICATION: As a leader, what changes are you facing in your life, in your church, or in your business? What changes should be implemented? Will you resist change or embrace it?

NOTES: _____

_____

_____

_____

_____

_____

_____

_____

_____

_____

Reflections on Your Leadership Journey

In the space below, record your reflections or thoughts
as you continue your leadership journey:

11.

LEADERS ARE WILLING TO ASSUME RISKS

Jehovah now instructed Moses, "Send spies into the land of Canaan—the land I am giving to Israel; send one leader from each tribe…" "[The spies reported that] the people living there are powerful, and their cities are fortified and very large; and what's more we saw Anakim giants there!" …But Caleb reassured the people as they stood before Moses, "Let us go up at once and possess it," he said, "for we are well able to conquer it!" "Not against people as strong as they are!" the other spies said. "They would crush us!"

Numbers 13:1-2; 28; 30-31 (TLB)

I can do all things in him who strengthens me.

Philippians 4:13 (RSV)

Be strong in the Lord, and in the power of his might.

Ephesians 6:10 (KJV)

Without some risk taking, new developments or innovations would seldom be accomplished. The great explorers and inventors were all risk takers.

Alfred Nobel finally invented dynamite, but in the process he blew up his house, his laboratory and his brother, Emil, before he was able to control his invention.

Successful leaders are willing to assume risks. Such is part of progress. However, effective leaders also know that such risks should be weighed carefully and one should not be foolhardy in the process. Alfred Lord Tennyson immortalized the 673 members of the British Light Brigade (light cavalry) in his famous poem, *The Charge of the Light Brigade*. The event, giving rise to this poem, occurred during the Crimean War, on September 26, 1854. The men of the Light Brigade dutifully followed their orders. As Tennyson describes the situation: *" 'Forward, the Light Brigade!'...Theirs not to reason why, Theirs but to do and die, Into the valley of Death rode the six hundred."* Unfortunately, the Light Brigade never had a chance. In a foolhardy act, its commanding officer ordered the Light Brigade to charge a Russian force of 12,000 soldiers who were supported by artillery. It is amazing that only 247 men of the Light Brigade were killed or wounded. Tennyson describes the outcome: *"Then they rode back, but not, Not the six hundred."*

The story is told about Dr. Evan O'Neill Kane, a successful surgeon, who for years had considered the possibility of using local anesthetics in areas where a general anesthetic had traditionally been used. He was eager to determine whether an appendectomy could be performed using only a local anesthetic. He was confident that it could be done, but could not find anyone willing to stay awake through such a surgery. However, on February 15, 1921, he found a willing patient. Dr. Kane removed the patient's appendix, the patient felt no pain, and recovered without any complications. The operation was considered to be a success. Who was the patient who was willing to take such a risk? It was none other than Dr. Kane, himself, who had removed his own appendix using a local anesthetic. It was a risky move on Dr. Kane's part, but a risk he was willing to take.

Sir Christopher Wren, the renowned architect whose buildings include St. Paul's Cathedral, once designed and supervised the building of a large church dome without supporting pillars. In spite of Wren's protests, the authorities responsible for the building demanded that two supporting pillars be added to keep the dome from collapsing. Some 50 years later, the dome was being repainted and scaffolding was built to provide access to the dome. The workers made an amazing discovery—the two pillars that had been added didn't touch the ceiling—they were short by some two feet and supported nothing. Wren's decision to not have the pillars support the ceiling was a calculated risk, but one he was willing to take because of the confidence he had in his own design and in his ability and skill as an architect.

Not all efforts and risks taken result in immediate success. If one doesn't first succeed, he or she is probably about average. A credo for effective leaders has been: "Either lead, follow, or get out of the way!" Progress cannot be attained without some risk. But those who are willing to take risks also reap the rewards.

Perhaps the following poem places the subject of "risk" in its proper perspective:

> *To laugh is to risk appearing the fool.*
> *To weep is to risk appearing sentimental.*
> *To reach out for another is to risk involvement.*
> *To expose feelings is to risk exposing our true self.*
> *To place your ideas, your dreams, before the crowd*
> *is to risk loss.*
> *To love is to risk not being loved in return.*
> *To live is to risk dying.*
> *To hope is to risk despair.*
> *To try at all is to risk failure.*
> (Author Unknown)

In the 13th chapter of Numbers, only two of the spies (one of whom was Caleb and the other was Joshua) sent into the land of Canaan were willing to risk crossing the Jordan River and possessing the land promised to them by God. They were right and the other ten were wrong. Those other ten were not allowed to cross the Jordan and enter the Promised Land.

APPLICATION: Are you willing to take a calculated risk? What opportunities have you lost in the past because you refused to take a risk? What risks do you currently see in the future of your church, your business, or other endeavors?

NOTES: _____

_____

_____

_____

_____

_____

_____

_____

_____

12.

LEADERS USE A WILDERNESS EXPERIENCE FOR GROWTH AND DEVELOPMENT

And it came to pass in those days, when Moses was grown, that he went out unto his brethren; and looked upon their burdens: and he spied an Egyptian smiting an Hebrew, one of his brethren....he slew the Egyptian, and hid him in the sand....now when the Pharaoh heard this, he sought to slay Moses. But Moses fled from the face of Pharaoh and dwelt in the land of Midian....

Exodus 2:11-12; l5 (KJV)

History reveals that a number of great leaders have had wilderness experiences. In the context of this book, a "wilderness experience" is a period of separation or exile. Such an experience can be either literal or figurative.

Moses, although an adopted prince of Egypt, was exiled into the wilderness by Pharaoh after he had killed an Egyptian who was beating a Hebrew. At 40 years of age, many would have thought that, as a leader, Moses was all washed up. However, it was in the wilderness that Moses found God and God had new leadership plans for Moses. His wilderness experience prepared him to lead the Hebrew slaves out of Egypt and for another 40 years of survival in the "wilderness."

A "wilderness experience" can be a time for growth and development out of which a leader emerges with renewed strength, maturity, and focus.

King David used his wilderness experience, consisting of some 15 years, as a period of growth and maturity which better prepared him to assume his role as the greatest of the kings of Israel.

Franklin D. Roosevelt used the "wilderness experience" that followed a crippling attack of polio to read books on geography and other enlightening publications which later proved beneficial. Some had predicted that Roosevelt's political career was over. However, not allowing the crippling effects of polio to deter him, he was elected President of the United States. Later, in particular, his geographical knowledge of the world's areas affected by World War II was a subject of amazement to his advisors.

Winston Churchill was a political exile as an outspoken critic of Adolph Hitler and as a vocal opponent to Great Britain's position of pacifism. However, when the time came, Churchill was ready to assume his role as the one who would lead England during its greatest time of peril—"a time to try men's souls."

After Sam Houston was forced out as the governor of Tennessee, he went into a self-imposed exile in the wilderness where he lived with the Cherokee Indians. Later, he had the strength and resolve to lead the new Republic of Texas as it declared its independence from Mexico. He became its first elected president, guided it into statehood, and later served as a United States senator and as a two-term governor of the State of Texas.

Nelson Mandela served 27 years in prison under South Africa's apartheid rule. He then went on to lead all of the people of South Africa, black and white, as its President, following the abolishment of apartheid.

The question is not, why has God placed me in this "wilderness?" But, rather, what is God trying to teach me as a result of this experience?

A wilderness experience can destroy a person or it can provide a time for growth and development whereby the leader can renew his or her strength and resolve to achieve great accomplishments. Often it is the place where one can renew and/or find a right relationship with God. As Isaiah the prophet said, "But they that wait upon the Lord shall renew their strength. They shall mount up as if with wings of eagles; they shall run and not be weary; they shall walk and not faint" (Isaiah 40:31 TLB).

APPLICATION: Have you had a wilderness experience? If not, are you prepared to survive such an experience through growth and development and a renewal of your relationship with God?

NOTES: _____
_____
_____
_____
_____
_____
_____
_____
_____

Reflections on Your Leadership Journey

In the space below, record your reflections or thoughts
as you continue your leadership journey:

13.

LEADERS VIEW THEIR EXPERIENCES AS SYNERGISTIC

At this time Moses was born, and was beautiful before God. And he was brought up for three months in his father's house; and when he was exposed, Pharaoh's daughter adopted him and brought him up as her own son. And Moses was instructed in all the wisdom of the Egyptians, and he was mighty in words and deeds.

Acts 7:20-22 (RSV)

"I am Joseph, your brother whom you sold into Egypt.... God has sent me here to keep you and your families alive, so that you will become a great nation.... And he has made me a counselor to Pharaoh, and manager of this entire nation, ruler of all the land of Egypt."

Genesis 45:4-b; 7-8 (TLB)

And we know that all that happens to us is working for our good if we love God and are fitting into his plans.

Romans 8:28 (TLB)

A synergism is generally defined as a result that is greater than the sum total of its parts. The experiences of leaders—both good and bad experiences—can have an end result that enables a person to become a better leader and to accomplish more than if he or she had not had those experiences.

Thus, whether we like it or not, we are the sum total of our experiences. These experiences serve to mold us and shape us into the person we have become. All such experiences can be used for our good if we love God and are willing to fit our lives into his plan.

Moses was chosen by God to lead the Hebrew people out of the bonds of slavery in Egypt. At that time, Moses was 80 years of age. The first 40 years of his life were lived in the palace of the Pharaoh as an adopted son of Pharaoh's daughter. After being exiled by Pharaoh, he lived his next 40 years in the desert wilderness tending to the flocks of his father-in-law, Jethro. Thus, he had been schooled in the ways of the Egyptians and knew the ways of the desert as well. Who could be better prepared for God to use to free a people who would live for 40 years in the desert. His experiences were synergistic.

In today's vernacular, Joseph would be considered a "smart-alecky kid" who was his father's "pet." He didn't have to work like his older brothers and flaunted his "coat of many colors." His brothers feigned his death and sold him to a caravan of Ishmaelite traders on their way to Egypt. In Egypt, Joseph became a slave and a trusted administrator to Potiphar, the captain of the palace guard, until he was wrongly accused and thrown into prison. However, because of his positive attitude and his resourcefulness, the chief jailer handed over the entire prison administration to Joseph. As one who could interpret dreams, he ultimately found favor with Pharaoh, who had a reoccurring dream that no one else could interpret (note that Joseph gave God credit for his ability to interpret Pharaoh's dream). All of these experiences were synergistic and served to prepare Joseph for a leadership position that would enable him to save his family and all of Egypt when a famine came upon the land.

Sam Houston is remembered primarily as a Texas hero, who led the army that defeated the Mexican general, Antonio Lopez de

Santa Anna, and who later became Texas' first elected president. Prior to coming to Texas, Sam Houston had served as an officer under General Andrew Jackson during the war of 1812 and as a major general in the Tennessee militia. He also had served as a member of Congress from Tennessee, governor of Tennessee, and the ambassador to the United States from the Cherokee Nation. All of these experiences prepared him for his new role as leader of the fledgling Texas Republic in 1836. His experiences were synergistic.

Abraham Lincoln, who some regard as the greatest President of the United States, had many experiences both good and bad, all of which served to prepare him to lead this country during one of its darkest periods. Not all of his experiences could be considered successful or positive. They included: failing in business at age 22, being defeated in his bid for the legislature at age 23, experiencing the death of his sweetheart at age 26, suffering from a nervous breakdown at age 27, being defeated for Congress at ages 34 and 39, being defeated for the Senate at ages 46 and 49, and being defeated for Vice President at age 47. Lincoln was a practicing lawyer and understood the frontier people who comprised the "grass roots" of this county. Because of his failures, he also acquired the leadership characteristic of humility. At age 51, he was elected President of the United States. God used Lincoln's synergistic experiences to prepare him to lead the Union during the Civil War.

The Apostle Paul was born a Roman citizen but was a member of the tribe of Benjamin. Although born in the Greek city of Tarsus, he was brought up in Jerusalem and studied at the feet of Gamaliel, the most illustrious rabbi of that day (see Acts 5:34). He was an expert in the Jewish law. After his conversion, Paul used his understanding of the Hebrew Scriptures to make the transition in his understanding of the Gospel of Jesus. His letters, combined with the Gospels, became the foundation of the Christian movement. All of his experiences as a Hebrew scholar, a persecutor of the early church, being struck blind on the way to Damascus, and being shipwrecked, beaten, and jailed, served as a synergism of the end result—a servant of God and a leader of the Christian Church.

As leaders, we should view all of our experiences as synergistic. At the time we go through a particular experience, we may ask,

"Why me, Lord?" However, we must look past each particular, and perhaps seemingly unpleasant, experience and remember that all things work for our good if we love God and are applying these experiences to His plan for our lives.

APPLICATION: What experiences have you had that were synergistic? Name one person who has lived during your lifetime who you believe exemplifies the principle of synergistic leadership. How do you plan to apply this synergistic principle to your own leadership abilities?

NOTES: _____

_____

_____

_____

_____

_____

_____

_____

_____

14.

LEADERS KNOW HOW TO HANDLE POWER

◦❯❯══◉══❮❮◦

*"You shall die, Ahimelech, along with your entire family!"
the king shouted. He ordered his body-guards, "Kill these
priests, for they are allies and conspirators with David...."
But the soldiers refused to harm the clergy. Then the king
said to Doeg, "You do it." So Doeg turned on them and
killed them, eighty-five priests in all, all wearing the
priestly robes. Then he went to Nob, the city of the priests,
and killed the priests' families—men, women, children,
and babies, and also all the oxen, donkeys, and sheep.*

1 Samuel 22:16-20 (TLB)

*It happened, late one afternoon, when David arose from
his couch and was walking upon the roof of the King's
house, that he saw from the roof a woman bathing; and
the woman was very beautiful. And David sent and
inquired about the woman. And one said, "Is not this
Bathsheba, daughter of Eliam, the wife of Uriah the
Hittite?" So David sent messengers, and took her; and she
came to him, and he lay with her.*

2 Samuel 11:2-4a (RSV)

Then the king wrote to his whole kingdom that all should be one people, and that all should give up their particular customs... Many even from Israel gladly adopted his religion; they sacrificed to idols and profaned the Sabbath.... He added, "And whoever does not obey the command of the king shall die."

1 Maccabees 1:41-43; 50
(RSV, Apocrypha)

Lord John Emerich Acton, the English historian, in a letter to Bishop Creighton in 1887, is quoted as saying, "Power tends to corrupt and absolute power corrupts absolutely."

History is replete with examples of those who have ascended to positions of power and who have allowed such power to totally corrupt them. Most have been tyrants and considered themselves to be above the laws of man and God.

In First Samuel 22, we find King Saul ordering the killing of God's innocent priests along with their families and livestock. Because of his hatred of David, Saul used his power as king to order the unwarranted death of these innocents.

Likewise, David, as king of Israel, had absolute power over all of his subjects in the kingdom. And while David is viewed as a great leader and one who had found favor with God, in one instance he used his power to take the wife of another even though he had many wives. Also, prior to sending for Bathsheba, David was told that she was "the wife of Uriah the Hittite." How could Bathsheba refuse the king—one who held the power of life and death? David's abuse of power was compounded further when he tried to "cover up" his actions by ordering his general to place Uriah in the heat of battle where he would surely be killed.

The Apocryphal books of First and Second Maccabees, describe the terrible acts of the tyrant Antiochus Epiphanes IV (which were prophesied in the Book of Daniel 8:24, 9:23, and 12:11). Antiochus desecrated the altar of the burnt offerings in the Temple in Jerusalem. He forced the Jews to participate in heathen activities and put to death all who were caught with the Book of the

Law in their possession. It is said that Antiochus Epiphanes IV had a tendency to cruelty that bordered on madness. He was ultimately overthrown by a revolt led by Judas Maccabeus in December 164 B.C. This victory is celebrated today by the Jews as Hannukkah, or the Festival of Lights.

In more modern times we have seen those corrupted by absolute power. Examples include Hitler, Mussolini, and Stalin, among others. Their acts of cruelty and genocide are familiar to almost every American.

More recently, the news has been filled with reports of the actions of Saddam Hussein, the former dictator/president of Iraq. Along with his cruel sons, he committed numerous atrocities against various groups within Iraq to include the Kurdish people. It has been estimated that Saddam Hussein was responsible for the death of 300,000 of his own people. In December, 2002, he said in an address read on television that the Iraqis were ready to fight a "holy war" against the United States. He refused to cooperate fully with United Nations weapon inspectors, although, subsequently, nuclear and biological weapons were not found by the occupying coalition forces. On December 20, 2003, following Saddam's capture, Ghassan Charbel, a columnist for the Arabic-language *Al Hayat* newspaper, described Saddam Hussein as follows: "He is the man who killed his nation twice, once in his ruling days and again the day his recklessness facilitated the occupation of his country."[5] Power had corrupted Saddam Hussein to the point where he was devoid of rational thought and blind to reality.

Richard M. Nixon thought that his power as President could allow him to defy an order from a United States District Judge regarding certain "White House-tapes." Such thinking destroyed what could have been the culmination of a long career as a leader and statesman.

Historians have indicated that, if Adolph Hitler had died during the middle 1930s, he could have gone down in history as a great statesman who revitalized the German economy. However, his corruption by power, coupled with his personal hatred for the Jews, caused the name of "Hitler" to become the personification of evil.

Corruption resulting from power is seen in the executive offices in modern corporations. Executives who treat public corporations like they are their own personal "piggy banks" are examples of the abuse of power. The news reports of such activities are numerous and include the actions of executives from WorldCom, Enron, and HealthSouth, just to name a few.

On perhaps a more familiar level, abuse of power is found in the supervisory and middle management levels of many modern organizations. Abuses of power manifest themselves in such areas as sexual harassment and discrimination in hiring and promotions. Too often, long-term managers at all levels become entrenched in positions of authority which leads to the abuse of the power granted to them.

Thus, leaders must realize that power is a gift and must be treated accordingly. Power comes from the governed in governments, from the shareholders in corporations, and from the members in churches and non-profit organizations. When power does corrupt, some brave person occasionally speaks out and discloses the problem. In 2002, *Time Magazine* chose as its "Persons of the Year" three women who reported wrongdoing and/or corruption within their organizations: FBI agent Coleen Rowley, WorldCom auditor Cynthia Cooper, and former Enron vice president Sherron Watkins.

Effective leaders must learn how to handle power appropriately so as to avoid the potential corruption that is concomitant with such power.

APPLICATION: Who do you know who has used power wrongly? Name some instances where absolute power has led to the corruption of its possessor. What will you do to assure that you will not abuse the power granted to you as a leader?

NOTES: _____

_____

_____

_____

_____

Reflections on Your Leadership Journey

In the space below, record your reflections or thoughts
as you continue your leadership journey:

15.

LEADERS DO NOT CELEBRATE OVER THE FALL OF AN ENEMY

<><=◎=><>

Do not rejoice when your enemy falls, and let not your heart be glad when he stumbles.

Proverbs 24:17 (RSV)

Then David and all the men with him took hold of their clothes and tore them. They mourned and wept, and fasted until evening for Saul and his son Johnathan, and for the army of the Lord and for the house of Israel, because they had fallen....

2 Samuel 1:11-12 (NIV)

If anyone had a reason to celebrate over the fall of an enemy, it was David after learning of the death of Saul. Saul had relentlessly pursued David with the intent to kill him. Saul had forced David to become a fugitive living in the wilderness and in caves.

Thus, one would think that David would celebrate upon hearing the news that his long-time enemy had been killed. With Saul's death, David could assume his rightful place as the anointed king of Israel.

However, rather than an act of celebration, David and his band of men went into mourning. David "rent" his clothes and he and his men (who, likewise, had been pursued by the army of Saul) "mourned and wept, and fasted until evening for Saul...."

Shouldn't the occasion of the fall of an enemy be a time for celebration? A fall of our enemy may not be the result of his or her death but could also mean that the person has been removed from his or her position of authority or otherwise has been humiliated or disparaged for some transgression. How should a leader react?

General Ulysses S. Grant, after accepting the surrender of the Confederate Army from General Robert E. Lee, later reflected on his feelings:

> *I felt like anything rather than rejoicing at the downfall of a foe who had fought so long and valiantly.... When news of the surrender first reached our lines our men commenced firing a salute of a hundred guns in honor of the victory. I at once sent word, however, to have it stopped. The Confederates were now our prisoners, and we did not want to exult over their downfall.*[6]

During World War II, General George S. Patton, Jr., was kept out of action as a result of a "slapping incident" involving a soldier who was suffering from battle fatigue but who had no apparent physical injuries. General Eisenhower ordered Patton to make the rounds of every Seventh-Army unit and apologize for the incident. Patton was then assigned to a command in England and removed from action until January, 1944. Many who served with Patton idolized him and he has been referred to with great praise by military historians. General Lucian Truscott called him, "...the most outstanding battle leader of World War II." But Patton, an outspoken and controversial figure who had made enemies during his rise through the ranks, became a prime target for his critics following the "slapping incident." Numerous military, government, and civilian leaders used this incident to criticize Patton and to gloat over his public humiliation.

When Richard M. Nixon resigned as President of the United States, many celebrated his fall from grace. Nixon was the only President in the history of this country to resign from office.

Quickly forgotten, in the midst of the voice of critics, were those important accomplishments which he had made during a period of leadership spanning many years as a governor, a congressman, Vice President, and President.

In the church, we see leaders falling from grace from time-to-time. The reaction is generally one of "he got what he had coming to him." And even those, who may not outwardly voice their satisfaction of such a fall, secretly rejoice it in their hearts.

It has been said that the "*army of God* too often shoots its own wounded." Rather than seeking a restorative relationship with a fallen brother or sister, Christians too often rejoice over a fellow Christian's fall from grace. Of course, Satan wants our brothers and sisters to stumble, since any criticism of the church works to his advantage.

When we as Christian leaders celebrate over the fall of one who may have been perceived as our enemy, we aid Satan in his goal of disparaging the church and its leaders.

Effective leaders know that revenge and hatred is counterproductive. Rather than "shooting the wounded," leaders should seek to heal them and to forgive as Christ has taught us to do.

APPLICATION: Whether in business, government, or the church, we should mourn when a leader falls. Even if that one is thought to be our enemy, we should remember and practice the teachings of Jesus when He said, "Love your enemies and pray for those who persecute you" (Matthew 5:44 RSV). Can you forgive your enemies?

NOTES: _____

_____

_____

_____

_____

_____

_____

Reflections on Your Leadership Journey

In the space below, record your reflections or thoughts
as you continue your leadership journey:

16.

LEADERS REALIZE THAT ARROGANCE LEADS TO DISASTER

◄►═◑═►►

James and John, the sons of Zebedee, came forward to him and said to him, "Teacher, we want you to do for us whatever we ask of you." And he said to them, "What is it you want me to do for you." And they said to him, "Grant us to sit, one at your right hand and one at your left, in your glory." …When the ten heard this, they began to be angry with James and John.

Mark 10:35-37; 41 (NRSV)

History indicates that, over a period of time, leaders may develop the character flaw of arrogance. Perhaps this is a feeling of pride or haughtiness that is the result of one's position of authority.

Saul is a good example of how arrogance can creep into one's life if not continually held in check. Three particular examples of arrogance are reflected in the life of Saul—all of which strongly contributed to his ultimate downfall.

The first incident took place when Saul became impatient and did not wait for Samuel the prophet to prepare a sacrifice prior to Saul's leading his army into battle with the Philistines (1 Samuel 13:8-14). Saul took matters into his own hands and assumed the role of priest, along with that of king, by officiating over the sacrifice himself. The second incident was when Saul lied to Samuel the prophet after Saul had disobeyed the command of God to destroy the Amalekites, including all of their herds (1 Samuel 15:2-3, 9; 19-23). The final act of total arrogance occurred when Saul sought advice from the Witch of Endor after he had banned witches and fortune-tellers from Israel (1 Samuel 28:7-12).

Arrogance is often the result of pride, a belief that we are in charge rather than God being in charge. James and John were arrogant when they sought the two highest positions among the disciples to the exclusion of the others. Jesus used this act of arrogance to teach them the importance of "servant leadership" saying, "The kings of the Gentiles exercise lordship over them; and those in authority over them are called benefactors. But not so with you; rather the greatest among you become as the youngest, and the leader as one who serves" (Luke 22:25-26 RSV).

King Henry VIII of England was arrogant when he couldn't have his way when trying to receive a papal annulment of his marriage to Catherine of Aragon. He declared the Church of England as being separate from the Holy Roman Catholic Church, appointed himself as head of the church, and executed those who stood in his way, including the Lord Chancellor, Sir Thomas More (More was subsequently canonized and is now known as St. Thomas More).

When Sewell Avery, the C.E.O. of Montgomery Ward, refused to relinquish his position and office after being fired by the board of directors, he was carried out of Montgomery Ward's office building, while still sitting in his executive chair, and thrown into the street.

An effective leader realizes that arrogance leads to disaster and, therefore, tempers his or her authority with humility. The effective leader realizes that his or her leadership position depends upon God's blessing and not strictly on the leader's own ability or authority. As the proverb says, "Pride goes before destruction, and a haughty spirit before a fall" (Proverbs 16:18 TLB).

APPLICATION: When have you observed an arrogant leader? How did you feel about him or her? Did your opinion of him or her change? As a leader, what action will you take to avoid the pitfalls associated with arrogant behavior?

NOTES: _____

_____

_____

_____

_____

_____

_____

_____

_____

Reflections on Your Leadership Journey

In the space below, record your reflections or thoughts
as you continue your leadership journey:

17.

LEADERS UNDERSTAND THE QUALITY OF MERCY

⋯⇒⇐⋯

…a king…decided to bring his accounts up to date. In the process, one of his debtors was brought in who owed him $10,000,000. He couldn't pay, so the king ordered him sold for the debt, also his wife and children and everything he had. But the man fell down before the king, his face in the dust, and said, "Oh, sir, be patient with me and I will pay it all." Then the king was filled with pity for him and released him and forgave his debt. But when the man left the king, he went to a man who owed him $2,000 and grabbed him by the throat and demanded instant payment. The man fell down before him and begged him to give him a little time. "Be patient and I will pay it," he pled. But the creditor couldn't wait. He had the man arrested and jailed until the debt would be paid in full. Then the man's friends went to the king and told him what had happened. And the king called before him the man he had forgiven and said, "You evil-hearted wretch! Here I forgave you all that tremendous debt, just because you asked me to—shouldn't you have mercy on others, just as I had mercy on you?"

Matthew 18:23-33 (TLB)

The above Scripture is a parable of Jesus which illustrates forgiveness—not the forgiveness of God but, rather, of man's forgiveness of man.

Mercy is a quality that all effective and successful leaders should possess. In the Scripture from Matthew, Jesus presented a parable about a man who was forgiven for a tremendous debt, an amount equal to ten million dollars. However, the same man would not forgive another who owed him the small sum of only $2,000.

This parable brings to mind another teaching of Jesus, which is referred to as the "golden rule." To paraphrase this teaching, we should treat others in the same manner that we would want to be treated under the same or similar circumstances.

In today's competitive and fast-moving society, we often hear the maxim: "Don't get mad, get even!" Business decisions are frequently made based purely upon economic considerations with far reaching effects on employees, competitors, and society in general. A decision may be made to close a manufacturing plant and move the operation to another country where cheaper labor is available, resulting in huge layoffs. Many economic decisions adversely affect worker retirement funds and other previously promised fringe benefits.

Shrewd businessmen, using the advice and counsel of even more shrewd lawyers, are able to implement business strategies which leave large numbers of economically injured people in their wake.

Leaders find themselves in positions of power and authority where they have the opportunity to show mercy. The situation may involve the indiscretion of an employee, a lapse of trust, or an infraction of greater consequences. The leader has the opportunity to judge and determine if a person deserves another chance. Is mercy the answer, or swift and harsh "justice?" The following story illustrates such a situation:

A young employee secretly misappropriated several hundred dollars of his company's money. When the deed was discovered, the young man was told to report to the office of the senior vice president. As he went upstairs to the administrative office, he was heavy hearted. He had no doubt he would lose his job. He also feared the possibility that legal action might be taken against him. It seemed as if within a matter of seconds his whole world had collapsed.

Upon arriving in the office of the senior executive, the young man was questioned about the entire affair. He admitted to what he had done. The executive then surprised him by asking him this question, "If I keep you in your present position, can I trust you in the future?" The young man brightened and said, "Yes, sir! You sure can! I've learned my lesson."

The executive then said, "I'm not going to press charges and you can continue in your present responsibility." The young man expressed his gratitude, but the executive stopped his effusive statements by saying, "I think you ought to know that you are the second man in this company who gave in to temptation and was shown leniency. I was the first. What you have done, I did. The mercy you are receiving, I received. It is only the grace of God that can keep us both." [7]

The Bible provides many examples of mercy. The majority of these illustrate the mercy shown by God. And, of course, we understand God's mercy. But mercy takes on a different quality, one that is like God's when it is shown by man. Perhaps the most beautiful and eloquent example of man's "quality of mercy" was penned by William Shakespeare in the following, often quoted, example:

The quality of mercy is not strain'd
It droppeth, as the gentle rain from heaven
Upon the place beneath: it is twice bless'd;
It blesseth him that gives, and him that
takes;
'Tis mightiest in the mightiest; it becomes
The throned monarch better than his crown;
His sceptre shows the force of temporal
power,

The attribute to awe and majesty,
Wherein doth sit the dread and fear of kings.
But mercy is above this sceptred sway,
It is enthroned in the heart of kings,
It is an attribute to God Himself:
And earthly power doth then show likest
God's,
When mercy seasons justice.
Merchant of Venice. Act IV. Sc. 1

Leaders should be reminded of Proverbs 11:17 (KJV): "The merciful man doeth good for his own soul." As Jesus said from the Sermon on the Mount, "Blessed are the merciful, for they shall obtain mercy" (Matthew 5:7 RSV).

APPLICATION: When has someone showed you mercy? When did you show another mercy?

NOTES: _____

_____
_____
_____
_____
_____
_____
_____
_____
_____

18.

LEADERS EXHIBIT COURAGE

"Then I will go to the king, though it is against the law; and if I perish, I perish." Mordecai then went away and did everything as Esther had ordered him.

Esther 4:16b-17 (RSV)

"Be strong and of good courage; be not frightened, neither be dismayed; for the Lord your God is with you wherever you go."

Joshua 1:9b (RSV)

"Don't worry about a thing," David told him. "I'll take care of this Philistine!"... "When I am taking care of my father's sheep," he said, "and a lion or bear comes and grabs a lamb from the flock, I go after it with a club and take the lamb from its mouth. If it turns on me I catch it by the jaw and club it to death. I have done this to both lions and bears, and I'll do it to this heathen Philistine too...." Then he picked up five smooth stones from a stream and put them in his shepherd's bag and, armed only with his shepherd's staff and sling, started across to Goliath.

1 Samuel 17:32; 34-36; 40 (TLB)

Be of good courage, and he shall strengthen your heart, all ye that hope in the Lord.

Psalms 32:24 (KJV)

The Lord is my helper, and I will not fear what man shall do unto me.

Hebrews 13:6 (KJV)

The Bible is filled with many acts of courage. A leader must exhibit courage in the face of obstacles and set an example for his or her followers. Sir Winston Churchill said, "Courage is rightly esteemed the first of human qualities because it is the quality which guarantees all others."

Queen Esther risked her life to save her family (she was the adopted daughter of Mordecai, the Jew) as well as the Jewish population of Persia against the plotting of Haman, who was second only to the king. Showing great courage as well as tact and skill, Esther exposed the evil Haman's plot and true character to the king. Her petition was granted, Haman was hanged on the very gallows he had prepared for Mordecai, and the Jews were saved. Even today the Jews celebrate their deliverance at the Feast of Purim (Esther 9:26-32).

David, a young shepherd boy, was willing to fight the Philistine giant, Goliath, when all others in Israel, including King Saul, were afraid. Saul, who "stood head and shoulders above all others" in Israel, should have acted as Israel's champion against Goliath. But it was little David, who stood up to, and who was victorious over, the giant.

A leader must have the courage of his or her convictions. A leader must know when to speak out even when doing so would be to support an unpopular cause. A true leader cannot "wink" and look the other way when unethical practices are being followed or when wrongs are being perpetrated within his or her organization. Such unethical practices can include discrimination in hiring or promoting.

In today's business climate with the scandals of the "Enrons" and the "WorldComs," a leader must be ready to take a stand even when doing so may result in ridicule, in the loss of a job, or even in becoming socially unpopular among one's peers. The leader, who takes an unpopular stand because he or she believes it is the right thing to do, exhibits true leadership courage.

General Billy Mitchell believed that airpower was an important part of the military's preparedness and that a large, independent air force should be created. His superiors disagreed with his position. Nonetheless, Mitchell showed the courage of his convictions and it cost him his military career. He was court-martialed in 1925. History reflects that he was right.

The apostle Paul is a great example of courage—a courage that would not allow him to turn away from his "defined mission" to take the Gospel to the Gentiles. He describes some of his hardships in Second Corinthians 11:

> *I have worked harder, been put in jail oftener, been whipped times without number, and faced death again and again and again. Five different times the Jews gave me their terrible thirty-nine lashes. Three times I was beaten with rods. Once I was stoned. Three times I was shipwrecked.... I have faced grave dangers from mobs in the cities and from death in the deserts and in the stormy seas and from men who claim to be brothers in Christ but are not.*

It has been said that courage is what one calls on in spite of fear of danger or fear of failure. As Abraham Lincoln said in a speech: "The probability that we may fail in the struggle ought not to deter us from the support of a cause we believe to be just; it shall not deter me."[8]

History has proven that one person of courage can make a difference. If that one person has the required degree of courage along with the vision, the willpower, and the stamina to ignore overwhelming odds, he or she can make a difference. Examples of such persons include: Martin Luther; Abraham Lincoln; Mohandas Gandhi; Helen Keller; Susan B. Anthony; Winston Churchill; Martin Luther King, Jr.; and Nelson Mandela.

Conversely, if one does not have the courage to speak out, the results can be devastating. An example of this latter situation is described from the period immediately preceding World War II. The Rev. Martin Neimoeller, a German Lutheran pastor, was arrested by the Gestapo and sent to Dachau, a Nazi concentration camp, in 1938. He was freed by the Allied Forces in 1945, seven years later. He wrote the following piece entitled, "I Didn't Speak Up":

> *In Germany, the Nazis first came for the communists, and I didn't speak up because I wasn't a communist.*
>
> *Then they came for the Jews, and I didn't speak up because I wasn't a Jew.*
>
> *Then they came for the trade unionists, and I didn't speak up because I wasn't a trade unionist.*
>
> *Then they came for the Catholics, but I didn't speak up because I was a Protestant.*
>
> *Then they came for me, and by that time there was no one left to speak for me.*[9]

A leader must be ready to exhibit courage. Leaders can do so when they know they are right and that the Lord is on their side. As Paul said in his letter to the Philippians, "I can do all things through Christ who strengthens me" (Philippians 4:13).

APPLICATION: When have you exhibited courage? When have you remained silent when you should have spoken up? As a leader, how will you exhibit courage in the future?

NOTES: _____

_____

_____

_____

_____

_____

_____

19.

LEADERS SHOW COMPASSION

David reigned with justice over Israel and was fair to everyone. ...One day David began wondering if any of Saul's family was still living, for he wanted to be kind to them, as he had promised Prince Jonathan. He heard about a man named Ziba who had been one of Saul's servants, and summoned him.... "Yes," Ziba replied, "Jonathan's lame son is still alive." ...And from that time on, Mephibosheth ate regularly with King David, as though he were one of his own sons. Mephibosheth had a young son, Mica. All of the household of Ziba became Mephibosheth's servants, but Mephibosheth (who was lame in both feet) moved to Jerusalem to live at the palace.
2 Samuel 8:15; 9:1-2a, 3b, 11c-12 (TLB)

Finally, all of you, live in harmony with one another; be sympathetic, love as brothers, be compassionate and humble. Do not repay evil with evil or insult, but with blessing, because to this you were called so that you may inherit a blessing.
1 Peter 3:8-9 (NIV)

Compassion, as a leadership trait, may be viewed by some as a weakness. Compassion is the leader's ability to have feelings for another's hardship or sorrow that leads to some affirmative action on the part of the leader. Thus, the leader who has compassion does not merely have a feeling of sympathy for another person or situation; but, rather, implements a positive action to alleviate the perceived condition.

It was the custom in the ancient world to destroy one's enemies to include any heirs who might later prove to be a threat. Saul and his sons had pursued David with the intent to kill him. However, before they could harm David, Saul and his sons, including Jonathan, were slain by the Philistines (1 Samuel 31:1-2). Rather than expressing revenge or hostility, David had compassion on Jonathan's son, Mephibosheth, who was lame, and David treated him as if he were his own son. Compassion and kindness were qualities that set David apart as a leader in an otherwise cruel world.

The word compassion is said to be derived from two Latin words that mean "to suffer with." Thus, the leader who shows compassion has the ability to relate to the suffering of another.

Abraham Lincoln exemplifies the principle of compassion as a leader. Joshua Speed, who was said to be Lincoln's best friend, described him as a person who "had the tenderest heart for any one in distress, whether man, beast, or bird."[10] The story is told that Lincoln spent hours hunting for the nest of two young birds which the wind had blown out of a tree. Lincoln was quoted as saying, "I could not have slept well tonight if I had not saved those birds."[11] On another occasion, Lincoln delayed his journey to pull a stranded pig out of the mire. Many historians believe that, had Lincoln lived, the reconstruction of the South surely would have reflected his compassion.

General Omar N. Bradley recognized the importance of compassion in a leader. He is quoted as saying, "Far from being a handicap to command, compassion is the measure of it. For unless one values the lives of his soldiers and is tormented by their ordeal, he is unfit to command."[12]

When Nazi Germany was defeated during World War II, Harry S. Truman, as the new President of the United States, traveled to Germany to view the devastation first hand. There were those in the U. S. government who would have seen Germany remain a beaten and desolate people so that they could never rebuild and again become a military threat. However, Truman remembered what his grandmother had told him about the reconstruction period following the Civil War and how their family, as Confederate survivors, had suffered. Truman showed compassion for the German people and quickly approved a plan for the immediate reconstruction of West Germany.

President Franklin D. Roosevelt said, "Human kindness has never weakened the stamina or softened the fiber of a free people. A nation does not have to be cruel in order to be tough."[13] This same principle of compassion can be applied to individual leaders as well as to nations.

Perhaps the best example of compassion is found in the life of our Lord Jesus Christ. He had compassion on the multitudes because they were harassed and helpless, like sheep without a shepherd (Matthew 9:36). He healed the sick (Matthew 14:14), He fed the hungry (Matthew 15:32), He cured the leper (Mark 1:41), and He brought the dead back to life (Luke 7:13). Jesus even restored the ear of the High Priest's servant that was cut off by one of the disciples when the religious leaders were attempting to arrest Jesus (Luke 22:51).

As leaders, it is incumbent upon us to learn and practice the principle of compassion as we assume leadership positions in business, government, and the church.

APPLICATION: What examples can you give where leaders have exhibited compassion? Why do you believe that compassion is a strength rather than a weakness? How will you implement the principle of compassion in your role as a leader?

NOTES: _____

_____

_____

_____

_____

_____

_____

_____

_____

_____

20.

LEADERS ARE PATIENT

◈▸═▷ ◁═◂◈

We can rejoice, too, when we run into problems and trials for we know that they are good for us—they help us to learn to be patient. And patience develops strength of character in us....

Romans 5:3-4a (TLB)

There is a right time for everything.

Ecclesiastes 3:1 (TLB)

Patience can be defined as being willing to put up with waiting, i.e., a state of calm endurance without complaining or losing one's self-control. Unfortunately, being patient is not an easy thing for most of us.

When we think of patience in reference to the Bible, we usually think of Job. The "patience of Job" has become a part of our modern vernacular. However, there is not any Scripture in the Book of Job where it is specifically said that Job was patient. Most scholars believe that the term is derived from Job 2:10, where it is recorded, *"Shall we receive good at the hand of God, and shall we not receive evil?" In all this Job did not sin with his lips.* Although Job was going through a period of great suffering, he did not lose self-control or blame God for his problems. Thus, it would appear that Job exhibited the characteristic of patience.

Patience is not a characteristic usually found among the youth since most young people are impatient. Moreover, patience is a leadership principle that isn't learned easily and generally comes about as a result of maturity and experience. Some quotations regarding patience, from sources outside of the Bible, include the following:

> *He that can have patience, can have what he will.*
> *Benjamin Franklin*

> *Never think that God's delays are God's denials. Hold on; hold fast; hold out. Patience is genius.*
> *Comte Georges Louis Leclerc de Buffon*

> *It is not necessary for all men to be great in action. The greatest and sublimest power is often simple patience.*
> *Horace Bushnell*

> *Patience is power; with time and patience, the mulberry leaf becomes silk.*
> *Chinese Proverb*

The leadership principle of patience may also be viewed as one of "timing," i.e., a determination of the proper time frame in which to implement a particular action. This principle should be seen in contrast to impetuousness, which occurs when a leader acts hastily without proper planning or thought. Immature leaders, in particular, may react to a situation with what is often referred to as a "knee-jerk" reaction, rather than one which involves proper planning and a deliberate weighing of all of the facts at hand before making a decision.

However, patience should not be used as a mere excuse for delay when a critical action is called for. In such an instance, it becomes nothing more than procrastination. Unfortunately, leadership is often a matter of balancing timing within the constraints of the resources available, along with those external conditions which may affect the leader's decision-making. A leader must consider the distinct possibility that opportunities may be lost while he or she is waiting for "perfect conditions" which, in fact, may never come.

The Texas hero, General Sam Houston, was criticized during the Texas Revolution because he would not allow his army to directly attack the Mexican army led by General Antonio Lopez de Santa Anna. The Mexican army was superior in size and weaponry and, after a series of victories which included both the Alamo and Goliad, Santa Anna was confident that he could defeat Houston's poorly trained volunteer soldiers. Houston's army of Texians appeared to be running from Santa Anna (and Houston has been painted by at least one historian as a man of indecisions). Houston asked his soldiers to be patient and to wait for the right time to confront the enemy. History proves that Sam Houston was right. In the marshlands of San Jacinto, Houston decided that the time was right to attack. His small army defeated the much larger Mexican force in a victory that guaranteed the independence of Texas.

Peter was an impatient disciple and often spoke and acted impetuously. However, with maturity and an understanding of the Gospel of Jesus, he was able to assume the leadership of the early church (in Roman Catholicism, Peter is considered to be the first Pope).

It has been said that Abraham Lincoln "was a patient man, capable of bearing long delay and waiting for the right moment. He considered himself a patient man..."[14] But, Lincoln could also be assertive. It is said that he chose Ulysses S. Grant as his general because Grant, unlike General George McClellan, was as assertive as Lincoln perceived himself to be.[15]

The effective leader knows that patience is an important principle of leadership. Likewise, the effective leader knows that timing is equally important in determining when to implement his or her actions.

APPLICATION: Why should leaders learn the principle of patience? Name two modern leaders who exemplify the principle of patience in their leadership styles. How can you apply the principle of patience in your current position of leadership?

NOTES: _____

_____

_____

_____

_____

_____

_____

_____

_____

_____

21.

LEADERS HAVE A VISION

—•+—◗ ◖—+•—

Where there is no vision, the people perish...
                    Proverbs 29:18a (KJV)

...your old men shall dream dreams, your young men shall see visions.
                    Joel 2:28b (RSV)

Peter told them, "You know it is against the Jewish laws for me to come into a Gentile home like this. But God has shown me in a vision that I should never think of anyone as inferior."
                    Acts 10:28 (TLB)

I t can be said that successful leaders have been men or women of vision. Most leadership or management books address the subject of vision, which is usually thought to be similar to planning. However, having a vision is much more than mere planning alone.

Vision may be defined as *the ability to perceive, through one's imagination, a specific goal or objective that the leader believes to be both worthy and attainable.* Thus, such a vision on the part of the leader is a "future thing," something that is to take place in the future through the efforts of the leader and his or her followers.

Sometimes the word "dream" is used in place of the word "vision," as in the case of one's dreams or thoughts. When Martin Luther King, Jr., made his famous "I have a dream" speech, he was referring to his vision of how things could be without prejudice and segregation. He believed such a goal to be both worthy and attainable through his efforts and the efforts of his followers. Dr. King had become the leader of the civil rights movement in America and had accepted this leadership position in spite of great personal risk. On August 28, 1963, more than 200,000 people gathered at the nation's capitol on the mall between the Lincoln Memorial and the Washington Monument. King spoke these words to those who had assembled:

> *I have a dream that my four little children will one day live in a nation where they will not be judged by the color of their skin but by the content of their character.*
> *I have a dream today...where little black boys and black girls will be able to join hands with little white boys and girls and walk together as sisters and brothers....*
> *When...all of God's children, black men and white men, Jews and Gentiles, Protestants and Catholics, will be able to join hands and sing in the words of the old Negro spiritual...Thank God Almighty, we are free at last!*[16]

God gave Peter a vision that the Gospel was for the Gentiles as well as the Jews and that no person was inferior (Acts 10:28). This vision, that the Gospel should be made available to all people, was carried further by the apostle Paul who proclaimed, "There is neither Jew nor Greek, there is neither slave nor free, there is neither male nor female; for you are all one in Christ Jesus" (Galatians 3:28 RSV).

Leaders who have a vision make things happen by convincing their followers that their vision is worthy and attainable. Such leaders take their dreams, or visions, and forge them into reality. These visionary leaders take the merit of their cause, make it clear to others, and dedicate themselves to its worthiness until their vision reaches fruition. Examples of such leaders include the Wright brothers, Henry Ford, Fred Smith, and Bill Gates, among many others too numerous to list.

The Wright brothers had a vision that men could "fly in the air." Although others at that time in history viewed such a vision as preposterous, "the Wright brothers worked fervidly in their crowded bicycle shop, inspired and won followers, overcame obstacle after obstacle in their plan of progress, and finally succeeded in creating the first successful airplane."[17]

Fred Smith's vision was a courier service that could efficiently and effectively deliver letters and packages overnight throughout the United States. His vision became Federal Express.

Henry Ford's vision was to manufacture an automobile that every family could afford to own. His vision became the Ford Motor Company.

Bill Gates became the richest man in the world through the success of his company, Microsoft. His vision began when he was only a teenager. Gates writes in his book, *The Road Ahead*, about having a vision:

> *Back when I was a teenager, I envisioned the impact that low-cost computers could have. "A computer on every desk and in every home" became Microsoft's corporate mission, and we have worked to help make that possible. Now those computers are being connected to one another, and we're building software—the instructions that tell computer hardware what to do—that will help individuals get the benefits of this connected communication power.*[18]

Bill Gates' vision became such a driving force that he dropped out of Harvard University to make it a reality.

The leaders, who are mentioned above, were able to put their visions into words that became a "mission statement" for what they were seeking to accomplish. This written statement then became the proclamation by which their efforts and followers' efforts were guided.

The vision (mission) statement is "*what* you want to do, not *how* you're going to do it....It is not cast in stone; rather it is a living document, continually held before the organization, continually tested, and continually modified to adapt to changes..."[19]

Church leaders have come to recognize the importance of having a vision and writing vision statements. The Rev. Rick Warren is a strong proponent for the use of a vision statement and discusses its importance in his book, *The Purpose Driven Church*, which has become a model for church growth in the United States and beyond. Dr. Warren writes:

> *Most people think of "vision" as the ability to see the future. But in today's rapidly changing world, vision is also the ability to accurately assess current changes and take advantage of them. Vision is being alert to opportunities.*
>
> *...I outlined the vision I believed God had given me for Saddleback Church. The first task of leadership is to define the mission, so I tried to paint, in attractive terms, the picture as clearly as I saw it. Over the years we've returned again and again to that vision statement for midcourse corrections.*[20]

Because of Rick Warren's book and his many lectures (he has taught in seminars to over 22,000 pastors and church leaders from sixty denominations and forty-two countries) the "vision statement" has become an important leadership tool for many congregations. In progressive churches, vision committees have been formed, mission statements written, and objectives and goals formulated for the next five, ten, and twenty-five years.

If the church, or any organization, is to survive and prosper, its leaders must have a worthy and attainable vision.

APPLICATION: Name two or more modern leaders who you believe exemplify the leadership principle of "vision." Why do you think having a vision statement is important for an organization's success? How can you effectively utilize the leadership principle of "vision" in your own organization?

NOTES: _____

_____

_____

_____

_____

_____

_____

_____

_____

_____

Reflections on Your Leadership Journey

In the space below, record your reflections or thoughts
as you continue your leadership journey:

22.

LEADERS INSTILL CONFIDENCE

◆➤〓◉〓◆➤

So after Gideon had collected all the clay jars and trumpets they had among them, he sent them home, leaving only three hundred men with him.

Judges 7:8-9 (TLB)

So when the people heard the trumpet blast, they shouted as loud as they could. And suddenly the walls of Jericho crumbled and fell before them, and the people of Israel poured into the city from every side and captured it.

Joshua 6:20 (TLB)

To be effective, a leader must instill confidence in his or her followers—a confidence that this particular leader is one who can lead them to successfully achieve a predetermined goal or objective.

The leader who instills confidence is one who can inspire followers to follow him or her even though logical thinking might dictate otherwise. Two such leaders were Gideon and Joshua.

During the time of Gideon, the oppression of the Midianites

111

intensified against the tribes of Israel. Some 135,000 Midianites were camped in a nearby valley when Gideon assembled about 32,000 volunteer citizen soldiers. After dismissing the fearful and afraid, only 10,000 remained. At the direction of God, Gideon further reduced the number to a total of 300. The Midianites then outnumbered Gideon's army by some 450 to one. Nevertheless, the remaining 300 Israelites dutifully followed Gideon's instructions. At the appointed time, 300 trumpets blasted the air, 300 hands raised their pitchers and smashed them, 300 burning torches pierced the darkness, and 300 warriors cried out in a loud voice, "The sword of the Lord and of Gideon" (Judges 7:19-20 KJV). The result was that the enemies of Israel were completely routed and Israel's homeland was again secure.

Gideon was able to instill confidence in an army of only 300 brave warriors to follow his instructions in a battle against an army of 135,000 men.

Upon Moses' death, Joshua was chosen as his successor and led the Israelites to conquer the land promised to them by God. He convinced his army to march around the City of Jericho for seven days. On the seventh day, they marched around the city seven times. Following Joshua's instructions, on the seventh time the priests blew a long, loud blast and Joshua yelled to the people to "shout." And suddenly the walls of Jericho crumbled and fell before the army of Israel.

Joshua, as God's appointed leader, was able to instill in his army the necessary confidence to follow his orders.

An effective leader also instills confidence in his or her subordinates concerning their ability to succeed. This was one of the leadership principles that made General George S. Patton a successful leader. His subordinates had confidence in his ability. But, as a leader, he also demonstrated his confidence in them as well.

In 1898, Theodore Roosevelt, a lieutenant colonel in the United States Army, was able to instill confidence in an assembly of ragtag volunteers who became known as the "Rough Riders." Although primarily a group of cowboys and adventure seekers, they were able to defeat the Spanish army and capture Cuba during the Spanish-American War.

During the Great Depression and continuing during World War II, President Franklin D. Roosevelt was able to instill confidence in the American people through his series of "Fireside Chats." As the nation's leader, he convinced the American people that they could succeed in both economics and war and that they "had nothing to fear but fear itself." Sir Philip Sidney, the English soldier and states-man (1554-1586), has been quoted as saying, "I will either find a way, or make one." This is the type of confidence that inspires followers. A modern unit of the United States Air Force has adopted a variation of this quotation for their own motto: "Find a way or make one."

Joshua and Gideon had confidence because God was on their side. But as leaders, they had to instill that same level of confidence in their followers so they could have confidence in the established goals and objectives of the organization.

Leaders who inspire confidence are not limited to the battlefield but include the boardroom as well. This same leadership principle is applicable to all organizations including the church.

APPLICATION: Can you name a modern leader who instills confidence? What is there about a leader that instills confidence in his or her subordinates? What can you change about your leader-ship style that will enable you to instill confidence in others in order to accomplish the goals and objectives of your organization?

NOTES: _____

_____
_____
_____
_____
_____
_____
_____
_____

Reflections on Your Leadership Journey

In the space below, record your reflections or thoughts
as you continue your leadership journey:

23.

LEADERS ARE PERSISTANT AND DETERMINED

...To that end keep alert with all perseverance, making supplication for all the saints, and also for me, that utterance may be given me in opening my mouth boldly to proclaim the mystery of the Gospel...

Ephesians 6:18b-19 (RSV)

If you faint in the day of adversity, your strength is small.

Proverbs 24:10 (RSV)

[Jesus told this parable to his disciples to show them that they should be persistent] "In a certain town there was a judge who neither feared God nor cared about men. And there was a widow in that town who kept coming to him with the plea, 'Grant me justice against my adversary.' For some time he refused. But finally he said to himself, 'Even though I don't fear God or care about men, yet because this widow keeps bothering me, I will see that she gets justice, so that she won't eventually wear me out with her coming!'"

Luke 18:2-5 (NIV)

I can do all things in him who strengthens me.
Philippians 4:13 (RSV)

Successful leaders are a persistent and determined lot. Such leaders refuse to take no for an answer in the pursuit of their goal or objective. Their unofficial credo could well be *continue to press on.*

Such leaders appear to be tireless in their pursuit of what they have determined to be a worthy goal. In modern psychiatry, these leaders might be diagnosed as being somewhat "obsessive-compulsive." However, most candid observers would agree that persistence and determination are characteristics common to successful leadership.

The apostle Paul recognized the importance of determination and persistence as he pursued the goal of spreading the Gospel to the Gentile world. This objective included the founding of numerous churches and the establishment of pastors and leaders in those churches. Despite all the hardships he encountered (including jail, beatings, and shipwrecks), Paul was determined to continue his appointed work.

President Calvin Coolidge believed in the importance of persistence and determination and described such as follows:

Nothing in this world can take the place of persistence. Talent will not; nothing is more common than unsuccessful people with talent. Genius will not; unrewarded genius is almost a proverb. Education will not; the world is full of educated derelicts. Persistence and determination alone are omnipotent. The slogan "press on" has solved and always will solve the problems of the human race.

Persistence and determination are common threads found among the leaders in the Bible. Some Old Testament examples include Noah, Moses, Joshua, and David. New Testament leaders who showed persistence and determination include Paul, Barnabas, Peter, Silas, Timothy, James, and John.

Jesus instructed his disciples regarding the importance of

persistence in the parable of the persistent widow (Luke 18:1-8). Even an evil judge granted the petition of a widow who was persistent in her demands for justice. She was determined to obtain justice even from one who did not "fear God or care about men."

Perhaps one of the best modern examples of determination is found in the story of Irwin W. Rosenberg, a junior naval officer, who was discharged from military service after being diagnosed with cancer (which was standard military procedure at that time).

> *The loss of his job was quite a blow, but [Irwin] was determined to get back both his health and his job. With faith and dogged determination, he battled the disease that tried to take over his body. At one point, he was given only two weeks to live....*
>
> *Irwin then focused his attention on his desire to become a naval officer. He discovered, however, that regulations forbade reinstatement of a person discharged with cancer. Everyone told Irwin, "Give up. It would take an act of Congress to get reinstated." Their advice gave him an idea—he would pursue an act of Congress!*
>
> *President Harry S. Truman eventually signed into law a special bill that allowed Irwin W. Rosenberg to reenlist and [subsequently] become a rear admiral in the United States Seventh Fleet![21]*

Napoleon Bonaparte has been quoted as saying, "Victory belongs to the most persevering." Polybius, the Greek historian (c.120 B.C.), recognized the importance of determination and perseverance when he said, "Some men give up their designs when they have almost reached the goal; while others, on the contrary, obtain a victory by exerting, at the last moment, more vigorous efforts than before."

Noah was determined to build an ark on dry land. Moses was determined to lead the Hebrew children out of bondage in spite of the Pharaoh's objections. Joshua was determined to bring down the walls of Jericho. David was determined to defeat the Philistines and to unite the twelve tribes of Israel into a cohesive nation. Of course, all of these accomplishments were made possible with the blessings of God.

Therefore, the persistent and determined leader might do well to pray and seek God's blessing for his or her endeavor. Then, perhaps, God will grant the strength and energy and determination necessary to accomplish that goal. As Paul said in his letter to the Philippians, "I can do all things through Christ who strengthens me" (Philippians 4:13).

The Rev. Robert H. Schuller was determined to take $500.00 and an old drive-in threatre to subsequently create one of the largest and most influential churches in the world today. Dr. Schuller was persistent and determined even when the financial future appeared bleak and the nay-sayers were prolific.

Henry Wadsworth Longfellow put the concept of persistence and determination to verse when he wrote:

The heights by great men reached and kept
Were not attained by sudden flight,
But they, while their companions slept,
Were toiling upward in the night.

The effective leader recognizes the *Principle of Persistence and Determination* as an important part of his or her potential for success.

APPLICATION: How have you utilized the Principle of Persistence and Determination in accomplishing your leadership goals? What leaders have you observed who practice this principle? How can you apply this principle to your own organization in the future?

NOTES: _____

_____

_____

_____

Reflections on Your Leadership Journey

In the space below, record your reflections or thoughts
as you continue your leadership journey:

24.

LEADERS ARE DECISIVE

⋅⊹⋅═◑ ◐═⋅⊹⋅

What a shame—yes, how stupid!—to decide before knowing the facts!

Proverbs 18:13 (TLB)

If you wait for the perfect conditions you will never get anything done.

Ecclesiastes 11:4 (TLB)

"But if you are unwilling to obey the Lord, then decide today whom you will obey."

Joshua 24:15a (TLB)

Then the king said, "Let's get the facts straight: both of you claim the living child, and each says that the dead child belongs to the other. All right, bring me a sword." So a sword was brought to the king. Then he said, "Divide the living child in two and give half to each of these women!"

1 Kings 3:23-25 (TLB)

Leaders are required to be decision-makers. Leadership positions carry with them those responsibilities which require that decisions be made in a timely manner. Even by doing nothing, the leader has made a decision.

Decision-making is said to be the act of determining in one's own mind a course of action. For leaders, decisions are usually related to a problem, a difficulty, or a conflict which requires a resolution. Moreover, decision-making permeates all administrative activities, always involves judgment, and usually deals with future actions and values.

An effective leader will attempt to obtain accurate information upon which to base his or her decision. Unfortunately, most leaders do not have the luxury of waiting until they have all of the facts that might be available. Furthermore, there may well be conflicts concerning the accuracy of the available facts. Economics is a good example of this latter situation. Most respected economists seldom agree on a specific action to take even though they are using the same set of facts. As was mentioned in an earlier chapter, the management of Sears Roebuck and Montgomery Ward both had the same set of facts at their disposal following World War II. Each of their chief executives made a decision based upon these facts. History has proved that Sears Roebuck was right and Montgomery Ward was wrong.

As the writer of Ecclesiastes said, "If you wait for perfect conditions you will never get anything done" (Ecclesiastes 11:4 TLB). Unfortunately for the leader, there is seldom a totally right time to make and implement a decision.

During times of war, the military leader is forced to make a decision with whatever facts are available. In such cases, knowledge, experience, and intuition play an important role in the decision-making process. General George S. Patton, who was considered to be a decisive leader, was quoted as saying:

> *It is always important to know exactly what you are doing. The time to take counsel of your fears is before you make an important battle decision. That is the time to listen to every fear you can imagine! When you have collected all of the facts and fears, make your decision. After you have made your decision, forget all of your fears and go full steam ahead.*[22]

General George B. McClellan apparently was unable to make timely decisions. His overcautiousness prompted President Lincoln to remove McClellan from his command and to replace him with the more decisive General Ulysses S. Grant. Some historians believe that, if Lincoln had not replaced McClellan, the Union might have lost the Civil War.

Of course, the effective leader wants to obtain as much accurate information as possible prior to making his or her decision. Thus, a leader should never confuse decisive decision-making with hasty guesswork.

Often it is only in the reflective light of history that a decision is seen for what it really was. As Secretary of State, William Seward's decision to purchase Alaska from the Russians in 1867 was for many years referred to as "Seward's folly." However, history now reflects that it was a good decision for this nation. With the benefit of "20/20 hindsight," every leader could make good decisions.

King Solomon, in deciding which woman was the living baby's real mother, used wisdom as well as facts. Once he had announced that the baby was to be cut in half with each woman receiving half a baby, the real mother, out of love, asked that the baby be given to the other woman. Solomon was then able to make the correct decision concerning which woman should be awarded possession of the child.

Major decisions are never easy and such decision-making should not be approached lightly. In addition to knowledge, experience, facts, and intuition, it would serve the leader well to seek divine guidance through prayer before making a major decision.

Leaders may also want to seek the advice and counsel of others where time permits and where such "wise counsel" is readily available. However, in the final analysis, the decision must be made and the ultimate responsibility for such decision will rest with the decision-maker alone.

APPLICATION: If you used baseball standards to evaluate your "good" decisions, what would be your "batting average?" What modern leader would you classify as a good decision-maker? How can you improve the quality of your decisions?

NOTES: _____

_____

_____

_____

_____

_____

_____

_____

_____

25.

LEADERS ARE STEADFAST AND DEPENDABLE

Therefore, my beloved brethren, be steadfast, immovable, always abounding in the work of the Lord...
1 Corinthians 15:58 (RSV)

Work hard so God can say to you, "Well done." Be a good workman, one who does not need to be ashamed when God examines your work.
2 Timothy 2:15 (TLB)

...and he gathered up all the food of the seven years when there was plenty in the land of Egypt, and stored up food in the cities; he stored up in every city the food from the fields around it. And Joseph stored up grain in great abundance, like the sand of the sea, until he ceased to measure it, for it could not be measured.
Genesis 41:48-49 (RSV)

"You are Peter, a stone; and upon this rock I will build my church..."
Matthew 16:18a (TLB)

The term "steadfast" is found in the King James Version of the Bible with the Old English spelling, "stedfast." However, the meaning is the same. A leader who is steadfast is one who adheres firmly and faithfully to a principle or cause. Such a leader is firm, unchanging, and has his or her eyes fixed on a specific goal or objective.

The steadfast leader reflects an adherence to those principles which are developed through maturity and a grounding in biblical truths. A steadfast leader is one who is reliable and dependable—he or she has a standard of behavior that is ingrained within the leader and governs his or her actions.

Moreover, the steadfast leader is faithful and loyal to an organization, a group, or a cause.

When the steadfast leader accepts a commission, he or she can be relied upon to accomplish the assigned task. Moses was such a leader. During the last 40 years of Moses life, there was never a question where he stood on an issue. Moses was steadfast and dependable.

Joseph was such a leader. He was steadfast and dependable and the Pharaoh knew that he could depend on Joseph to accomplish the task at hand, i.e., to save the people from seven years of famine.

Joshua, too, was such a leader. After Moses' death, he led the Israelites to conquer the Promised Land, supervised the division of the territory among the twelve tribes, and led the people to renew their covenant with God. Joshua was steadfast and dependable. He stated his position plainly when he said, "…as for me and my house, we will serve the Lord" (Joshua 24:15 KJV).

Although Peter suffered many of the shortcomings associated with impetuous behavior, Jesus saw in him the qualities of a steadfast and dependable leader. Jesus chose Peter to be the "rock" upon which the new Christian church would be built (Matthew 16:18). Peter accepted the leadership role assigned to him. He was the first apostle to be called by Jesus (Matthew 4:18-20). His name heads every list of the Twelve in the New Testament. He served as spokesman for the disciples and was their recognized leader (Mark 1:36; Luke 22:32). The Book of Acts records that Peter continued to exercise a key leadership role in the early Church and the first eleven chapters of Acts are built around his activities as a leader. Peter was steadfast and dependable.

Daniel was steadfast and dependable. Even as a youth, he was determined to live by God's law although in a distant land (Daniel 1). His enemies even used his regularity at prayer to trap him in an attempt to turn the king against him. When the king had Daniel thrown into a den of lions, his miraculous survival resulted in a decree being issued by the king stating that all of the kingdom must "tremble and fear before the God of Daniel" (Daniel 6:26 RSV).

It was stated above that the steadfast leader is faithful and loyal. A biblical leader who violated the faith and trust placed in him was Joab, who was the general of King David's army. When ordered to place Uriah the Hittite at the front of battle (an act that would surely result in Uriah's death), Joab apparently did so out of his sense of loyalty and duty to the king. Later, however, Joab killed David's rebellious son, Absolom, even though David had ordered that Absolom not be killed (2 Samuel 18:5; 14-15). When David gave the command of the Israelite army to Amasa, Joab's cousin, Joab killed Amasa in an act of jealous hate. Joab also refused to accept Solomon as David and God's choice as David's successor and joined the cause of Adonijah (another of David's sons) against Solomon. Subsequently, Joab was killed in accordance with the deathbed wishes of King David, which David had given to Solomon (1 Kings 2:5).

In today's world, where insatiable greed and situation ethics abound, the effective leader needs to practice the Principle of Steadfastness and Dependability—he or she needs to be a leader who can be relied upon to accept and successfully complete a worthy goal when such is assigned.

APPLICATION: Are you a steadfast and dependable leader? If not, what can you do to develop this principle of leadership? Can you give examples of leaders who exhibit these characteristics?

NOTES: _____

_____

_____

_____

_____

_____

_____

_____

_____

_____

26.

LEADERS PRACTICE INTEGRITY

◆⇒〇⇐◆

"And how does a man benefit if he gains the world and loses his soul in the process?"
Mark 8:36 (TLB)

"Well done, good and faithful servant; you have been faithful over little, I will set you over much..."
Matthew 25:21 (RSV)

The Lord demands fairness in every business deal. He established the principle.
Proverbs 16:11 (TLB)

We can justify our every deed but God looks at our motives.
Proverbs 21:2 (TLB)

If a godly man compromises with the wicked, it is like polluting a fountain or muddying a spring.
Proverbs 25:26 (TLB)

When there is moral rot within a nation, its government topples easily; but with honest, sensible leaders there is stability.

Proverbs 28:2 (TLB)

Telling lies about someone is as harmful as hitting him with an axe, or wounding him with a sword, or shooting him with a sharp arrow.

Proverbs 25:18 (TLB)

In today's society, more than ever before, there is a need for our leaders to practice integrity. The use of the term "practice" may appear unusual in this context, if not out of place, when used with the word, "integrity."

However, after much reflection, the term "practice" may be the most appropriate term to use. Doctors practice medicine and lawyers practice law. Also, practice is defined as a "customary action or customary code of behavior." We practice in order to acquire proficiency, such as when we prepare for an athletic event or when we play a musical instrument. Moreover, the phrase, "put into practice," is used to describe the application of a set of principles or a particular philosophy.

The practice of integrity is not necessarily easy in today's world of situation ethics, behavioral rationalization, and circumstances which appear gray rather than black or white. Thus, the practice of integrity by a leader includes such terms as: fairness, faithfulness, fidelity, frankness, honesty, honor, justice, loyalty, morality, responsibility, righteousness, uprightness, and virtue.

Some of America's largest corporations have been affected by scandals at the highest level. These include Enron, WorldCom, and Tyco just to name a few. Impeachment proceedings against President Clinton and claims of impropriety among politicians have caused many to doubt the integrity of their leaders in the highest offices in the land. Even the church is not immune from situations which involve a lack of integrity.

The Bible is a guide for living a righteous life—one filled with integrity. The Book of Proverbs, in particular, provides us with many guidelines for walking the road of integrity.

God directed the prophet Ezekiel to indict Jerusalem and to publicly denounce her terrible deeds (Ezekiel 22:2). Such indictment was followed by a lengthy list of sins committed by the people. The leaders are described "[as] like wolves, who tear apart their victims, and they destroy lives for profit" (Ezekiel 22:27 TLB).

Fraud, greed, and dishonesty continued to be rampant in the Jerusalem of Jesus' day. Apparently, the high priest and the local money changers had conspired to declare that only the animals they sold were worthy of sacrifice in the Temple. The Gospel of John describes how Jesus, in an act of righteous anger against such dishonesty, made a whip out of ropes and drove the money changers out of the Temple (John 2:14-16).

The Book of Acts describes how Ananias and Sapphria attempted to deceive the early church leaders by donating the proceeds of the sale of their property. While they were not compelled to donate all of the proceeds from the sale, they lied anyway about the amount they were giving (Acts 5:1-2).

Among historical leaders, the words honesty and integrity have become synonymous with the person of Abraham Lincoln. Although some of the stories reflecting his honesty and integrity which followed Lincoln's death probably included some exaggerations or fabrications, it has been said that "enough of the stories were true that, long before his death, Lincoln had earned the name 'Honest Abe.' "[23] Some of our modern political leaders would do well to emulate Mr. Lincoln.

Whether involved in the church, a business, or government, those persons in leadership positions need to practice the principle of integrity. They need to be leaders to whom followers can look to for assurance that they are, in fact, practicing integrity.

There is no room for compromise in a leader's practice of integrity. As proverbs says, "If a godly man compromises with the wicked, it is like polluting a fountain or muddying a spring" (Proverbs 25:26 TLB). A compromise that dilutes the leader's honesty and integrity is unacceptable.

Stephen, the church's first martyr, was a man who would not

compromise as he stood with integrity before those accusers who had lied about him. Rather, Stephen accused them of their own misdeeds and pointed out their own lack of integrity. He asked them, "Which of the prophets did not your fathers persecute? And they killed those who announced beforehand the coming of the Righteous One, whom you have now betrayed and murdered" (Acts 7:52 RSV).

Sir Thomas More, the Lord Chancellor of England during the reign of King Henry VIII, disapproved of the king's divorce of convenience from Catherine of Aragon and refused to subscribe to the king's Act of Supremacy, the latter violating More's integrity. In order to save his life, all Thomas More had to do was pledge allegiance to the king and renounce Roman Catholicism. But More refused. As a result of this act of integrity, he was imprisoned and beheaded on a charge of treason (Thomas More was the subject of a motion picture, *A Man for All Seasons*, and was Canonized by the Roman Catholic Church in 1935).

Practicing integrity for the modern leader is not an easy matter. As one theologian put it, "Morality in the world today is upside down from the Word of God." The Christian leader must continually look to God's Word for direction in order to avoid being "poured into the world's mold of compromise and deceit" with its lure of personal gain.

Practicing integrity requires that we, as leaders, continually examine our relationships—specifically our relationship to *others*, to *God*, and to *ourselves*. And, if we, as leaders, find ourselves to have taken a detour, we must work to get back on the right road of integrity. Thus, periodically, as leaders, we must take a close look at ourselves and measure our integrity. Such introspection is exemplified in the poem generally referred to as "A Man in the Mirror."

> *When you get what you want in your struggle for self,*
> *And the world makes you king for a day,*
> *Just go to a mirror and look at yourself,*
> *And see what that man has to say.*
> *For it isn't your father or mother or wife,*
> *Whose judgment upon you must pass;*

The fellow whose verdict counts most in your life,
Is the one staring back from the glass.
Some people may think you are a straight-shooting chum,
And call you a wonderful guy,
But the man in the glass says you're a bum,
If you can't look him straight in the eye.
He's the fellow to please, never mind all the rest,
For he's with you clear up to the end,
And you have passed your most dangerous, difficult test,
If the man in the glass is your friend.
You may fool the whole world down your pathway of years,
And get pats on the back as you pass,
But your final reward will be heartache and tears,
If you've cheated the man in the glass.

—Anonymous

APPLICATION: Where do you rank the importance of integrity as a principle of leadership? Where have you seen integrity or a lack thereof exemplified among our leaders in business, government, and the church? How will you apply the Principle of Integrity in your role as a leader?

NOTES: _____

_____

_____

_____

_____

_____

_____

_____

_____

Reflections on Your Leadership Journey

In the space below, record your reflections or thoughts
as you continue your leadership journey:

27.

LEADERS KNOW THE IMPORTANCE OF TEAMWORK

-*»╾╾╾)(╾╾╾«*-

[Gideon] divided the three hundred men into three groups and gave each man a trumpet and a clay jar with a torch in it. Then he explained his plan. "When we arrive at the outer guard posts of the camp," he told them, "do just as I do. As soon as I and the men in my group blow our trumpets, you blow yours on all sides of the camp [break your clay jars] and shout, 'We fight for the Lord and Gideon!'"

Judges 7:16-18 (TLB)

As one writer put it, "No man is an island." If leaders are to accomplish worthy goals, they must do so through effective teamwork.

In order to be a leader, one must have followers. The leader and the followers, together, must form a cohesive team that can function as a single unit with the leader at its head. Thus, today, as in the past, a successful leader must be part of a committed leadership team.

Perhaps athletics can provide the best modern example of the importance of teamwork. In football, each team has a quarterback who is charged with the responsibility of calling the next play. Each of the eleven players has a specific assignment for each play called. If any one member of the team fails to perform his (and occasionally her) assignment, the play will not be successful.

Some years ago, the author played football on a team that could serve to illustrate the importance of teamwork:

> *This football team had one player who was an exceptionally talented athlete. That particular athlete, Wayne, was also talented in other areas as well. He was drum major of the school's marching band and played first-chair coronet. He caught the eye of the head football coach primarily because of his track and field achievements: he entered five district events—the hundred yard dash, low hurtles, broad jump, pole vault, and discus—and set five new district records. However, Wayne wasn't interested in playing football because, as drum major, he led the marching band during the half-time ceremonies.*
>
> *After much persistence, the head football coach convinced both the band director and Wayne that, if Wayne played football, he would be allowed to leave the game a few minutes before half-time, change into his drum major's uniform, and lead the band. After the half-time ceremonies, he could change back into his football uniform and rejoin the team.*
>
> *This arrangement worked well until the local newspaper ran a full page story about Wayne playing football and leading the band. Thereafter, the newspaper's sports reporters followed the football games closely and continued to extol Wayne's heroic exploits while seldom mentioning the names of the other members of the team. Several of the big linemen resented Wayne's publicity and decided to find out how great Wayne really was. During the next game, instead of blocking their opponents, they let the opposing team pour through the line leaving a vulnerable Wayne at the bottom of a heap of tacklers.*

The moral of this story is that even a great athlete, such as Wayne, needed everyone on the team to do his part. (Fortunately, the coach used his leadership skills and convinced everyone on the team that they needed to play like a team. The result was a district championship.)

It has been reported that a particular professional football player carries a card in his wallet bearing a quotation from Kipling's the *Law of the Jungle*: "For the strength of the pack is the wolf, and the strength of the wolf is the pack." It is true that wolves work together as a pack, but it is also true that there is always a leader of the pack. Only through teamwork is a wolf pack able to bring down the mighty caribou or the giant moose.

Gideon is an example of a leader who used teamwork to accomplish a great victory for God and Israel. Although outnumbered some 450 to one, Gideon divided his small army of 300 into three companies. Each man had a trumpet, a pitcher, and a torch. At Gideon's signal, 300 trumpets blasted the air, 300 hands smashed their pitchers, 300 burning torches pierced the darkness of the night, and 300 warriors cried out, "The sword of the Lord and of Gideon" (Judges 7:19-20 KJV). Gideon's use of precision teamwork on the part of 300 soldiers routed a Midianite army of 135,000. The Midianites were thrown into a state of panic, some killing their own comrades and others committing suicide. Because of Gideon's leadership and the effective use of teamwork, Israel was blessed with 40 years of peace.

Like all great military leaders, General George S. Patton recognized the importance of teamwork. Although a general is in command of an entire army consisting of hundreds of thousands, Patton "concerned himself with how the smallest unit, the squad, consisting of eight to twelve men, should be used. He stressed coordinated teamwork at all times."[24] In the motion picture, *Patton*, George C. Scott, in the role of General Patton, says, "[This] individuality stuff written about the Army in the *Saturday Evening Post* is a bunch of crap...An army is a team, it works as a team, eats as a team, and fights as a team."

Whether an organization consists of thousands, hundreds, or small numbers, the leader must assure that all members of the team are working harmoniously toward a common objective. To use two common analogies, everyone "must be on the same page" or everyone should be "singing from the same song sheet."

It has been said that, "All great leaders of the past and present have one thing in common: a leadership team that is loyal, motivated, collaborative, and knowledgeable."[25] Without teamwork, a leader's best efforts may well end in chaos and failure.

Thus, the effective leader must work to assure that the team members become a cohesive unit—one which works in concert. Each member of the team must be made to understand the "team process" while, at the same time, accepting and appreciating the individual differences of each team member. The leader will then be able to utilize teamwork to achieve the goals and objectives of the organization. If such is understood and implemented by the leader—like Gideon—the result can be victory and success.

APPLICATION: When have you observed effective teamwork in action? When have you been part of a team, either as a leader or a team member? How can and will you use teamwork to accomplish your organization's objectives?

NOTES: _____

_____

_____

_____

_____

_____

_____

_____

_____

28.

LEADERS RECOGNIZE TEMPTATION

And lead us not into temptation, but deliver us from evil.
Matthew 6:13 (RSV)

No temptation has overtaken you that is not common to man. God is faithful, and he will not let you be tempted beyond your strength, but with the temptation will also provide the way of escape...
1 Corinthians 10:13 (RSV)

It happened, late one afternoon when David...was walking upon the roof of the king's house, that he saw from the roof a woman bathing; and the woman was very beautiful. ...So David sent messengers, and took her; and she came to him, and he lay with her.
2 Samuel 11:2, 4a (RSV)

Now Joseph was handsome and good-looking. And after a time his master's wife cast her eyes upon Joseph, and said, "Lie with me." ...But he left his garment in her hand, and fled and got out of the house.
Genesis 39:6b-7, 12b (RSV)

So use every piece of God's armor to resist the enemy whenever he attacks, and when it is all over, you will still be standing up.

Ephesians 6:13 (TLB)

Leaders are faced with a myriad of temptations as they assume their leadership roles, whether they are in business, government, or non-profit organizations such as the church. One might say that temptation is everywhere.

Today's Christian leaders need a means of recognizing temptation when it appears and, secondly, a strategy for dealing with such temptation.

Temptation can be insidious—it can appear as "a wolf in sheep's clothing" so that the leader has difficulty seeing a particular temptation for what it really is. Thus, the leader must be ever vigilant. As the writer of First Peter warns: "[B]e vigilant; because your adversary the devil, as a roaring lion, walketh about, seeking whom he may devour" (1 Peter 5:8 KJV).

Leaders who have fallen prey to temptation have usually succumbed to the temptations of greed and/or sexual immorality. Although there are other temptations, these two appear to become the Achilles heel for many prominent leaders. The modern leader should be aware of the temptations generally referred to as the *Seven Deadly Sins*, which are: sloth, lust, anger, pride, envy, greed, and gluttony. One or more of these is usually responsible for a leader's fall from grace.

King David has been described as "a man after God's own heart." Yet, he was tempted when he saw Bathsheba bathing on the roof of her home. And, although he had many wives, he yielded to the temptation of lust and committed adultery with Bathsheba and, subsequently, murder when he had her husband, Uriah the Hittite, killed as part of a planned cover-up.

President William Jefferson Clinton succumbed to the sexual temptation of a pretty, young intern. He then denied it and attempted to cover it up. And, although he survived an impeachment proceeding, the one single event of the Clinton administration that stands out in the minds of many Americans is the "Monica Lewinsky Scandal."

Greed creates an opportunity for bad decisions on the part of leaders. Martha Stewart made a decision which involved her saving some $45,000.00 in the value of her ImClone Systems stock. She then attempted to cover up the fact that she had received a "tip" from her stockbroker. The result was the loss of millions of dollars in the value of the stock of her own company, a criminal conviction, and a prison term. The problem is that, more often than not, when the leader makes a bad decision its ramifications are far reaching and affect many people in addition to the leader, such as shareholders, employees, and others.

Such a situation is further illustrated in the case of Enron where both shareholders and employees suffered as the result of greed on the part of the corporation's top executives.

Political leaders and government officials, in particular, are subject to temptation in the form of bribes and other favors which would serve to compromise their integrity and oaths of office. When giving Moses advice regarding the selection of leaders, Jethro recognized this possibility by including the following admonition: "Find some capable, godly, honest men who hate bribes" (Exodus 18:21 TLB).

The Christian leader can choose from two courses of action when temptation raises its ugly head—*fight* or *flight*. In Ephesians 6, we are told to put on the whole armor of God and when the attack is over, we will still be standing. God's armor, which includes "the sword of the Spirit...[i.e.,] the Word of God" (Ephesians 6:17b TLB), will provide the means to fight if such is the leader's choice. However, in the case of sexual temptation, many spiritual leaders suggest that flight, not fight, is the proper course of action.

Joseph fled from the demanding advances of Potiphar's wife. Prior to fleeing, Joseph told her, "My master trusts me with everything in the entire household; he himself has no more authority here than I have! He has held back nothing from me except you yourself because you are his wife. How can I do such a wicked thing as this? It would be a sin against God" (Genesis 39:8-9 TLB).

Temptation often comes in the form of many disguises. Thus,

leaders must be perceptive and attempt to recognize temptation for what it is. When in doubt, ask God through prayer to grant wisdom, insight, and guidance that your decision will be a proper one. Paul ends his description of the *Whole Armor of God* with the following advice: "And pray in the Spirit on all occasions with all kinds of prayers and requests" (Ephesians 6:18a NIV).

In the fifth chapter of Ephesians, Paul provides a warning to the leaders of the church at Ephesus, "But among you there must not be even a hint of sexual immorality, or of any kind of impurity, or of greed, because these are improper for God's holy people" (Ephesians 5:3 NIV).

Thus, leaders must be able to recognize temptation when it appears and, moreover, be prepared to properly and effectively deal with it as well.

APPLICATION: Can you list several modern leaders who have succumbed to temptation? What was the result of their actions? As a leader, how can you recognize and avoid temptation?

NOTES: _____

_____

_____

_____

_____

_____

_____

_____

_____

29.

LEADERS HAVE SELF-DISCIPLINE AND SELF-CONTROL

❖⇒◯⇐❖

Every athlete exercises self-control in all things.
                                        1 Corinthians 9:25a (RSV)

Work hard and become a leader; be lazy and never succeed.
                                        Proverbs 12:24 (TLB)

You are a poor specimen if you can't stand the pressure of adversity.
                                        Proverbs 24:10 (TLB)

Look carefully then how you walk, not as unwise men but as wise, making the most of [your] time...
                                        Ephesians 5:15-16a (RSV)

Since an overseer is entrusted with God's work...he must be...one who loves what is good, who is self-controlled, upright, holy and disciplined.
                                        Titus 1:7a-8b (NIV)

But the fruit of the Spirit is...self-control....
Galatians 5:22a; 23a (RSV)

Self-discipline and self-control are combined as a single leadership principle since they are so closely intertwined in the leadership function. Self-discipline is that inner strength and resolve—a steeling of the will—that guides the leader in the conduct of his or her affairs. In comparison, self-control is the act, power, or habit of having one's faculties under control of one's own willpower.

As leaders, all of us have been given the same amount of time—24 hours per day, seven days per week, and 365 days per year. The way we utilize that time effectively is a matter of self-discipline.

Self-discipline includes the ability to maintain self-control when all others are "out of control." Adversity and crises are to be expected as part of one's leadership position. The ability to maintain control while handling such problems is the mark of the effective and successful leader. Rudyard Kipling describes such self-control in the following way:

If you can keep your head when all about you
Are losing theirs and blaming it on you;
If you can trust yourself when all men doubt you,
But make allowance for their doubting too;
If you can wait and not be tired by waiting,
Or, being lied about, don't deal in lies,
Or being hated don't give way to hating,
And yet don't look too good, nor talk too wise...
If you can think—and not make thoughts your aim,
If you can meet with Triumph and Disaster
And treat those two impostors just the same...
And so hold on when there is nothing in you
Except the Will which says... "Hold on!"[26]

The Apostle Paul, although imprisoned and shackled to one of the soldiers who guarded him in four-hour shifts, continued to receive visitors, preach the Gospel, and write letters to the various churches including the one at Ephesus (the letter to the Ephesians is one of those known as the "prison epistles"). Paul exercised self-discipline in the pursuit of his determined goal. And, during such adversity, Paul maintained his self-control.

Abraham Lincoln is an example of a leader who exhibited self-discipline. Gene Griessman describes this quality of Lincoln's as follows:

> *For Lincoln, self-discipline was inextricably linked to willpower. In a letter written two years before his election to the presidency, remembering a lifetime of commitment, Lincoln advised: "By all means, don't say 'if I can'; say 'I will.'"*[27]

Effective leaders must develop that level of self-discipline necessary to make the most of their time, i.e., to get more things done in the same 24 hours in each day that has been given to everyone else. John Wesley, the founder of Methodism, is an outstanding example of a person who achieved that level of self-discipline. The following is a description of Wesley's self-disciplined life:

> *Most people think of John Wesley as a powerful preacher, and, indeed he was. What many people do not know, however, is how prolific he was. He averaged three sermons a day for fifty-four years, preaching a total of more than 44,000 times in his life. In doing this, he traveled by horseback and carriage more than 200,000 miles—about 5,000 miles a year. For even a productive man, that would seem to be a full-time effort.*
>
> *Still, John Wesley found time to write and edit. His published works include a four-volume commentary on the entire Bible, a five-volume work on natural philosophy, a four-volume work on church history, and a dictionary of the English language. He also wrote histories of England and Rome, grammars on the Hebrew, Latin, French, and English languages, three works on medicine, six volumes of church music, seven volumes of sermons and controversial papers,*

and he edited a library of fifty volumes known as "The Christian Library."

He habitually rose at 4 AM and retired at 10 PM, allowing only brief periods for meals. Yet he declared, "I have more hours of private retirement than any man in England."[28]

The successful leader develops a level of self-discipline that results in his or her making time when there would appear to be none. Such a leader continues to lead with results time after time, year after year, in spite of adversity and crises.

Self-control requires the exercise and development of an inner strength. Just as one develops outer strength through exercise of the physical body, inner strength must be developed as well. As the apostle Paul prayed for "inner strength" in Ephesians 3:16, we, as leaders, must look to God for His help in building our inner person. The result can be that level of self-discipline and self-control needed to confidently face the adversity and crises which will ultimately come to those in leadership positions. Such self-control is available to us as a "fruit of the Spirit" (see Galatians 5:22-23 RSV).

Leaders need to be aware that crises are inevitable and often come when unexpected. As the late statesman Mike Mansfield said, "The crisis you have to worry about most is the one you don't see coming." These are the occasions when leaders need self-control and self-discipline.

Moreover, the successful leader must utilize self-discipline to establish priorities and to allocate the necessary time to accomplish those priorities. As one such leader was heard to remark in jest, "There are 24 hours in a day; and then there are nights."

APPLICATION: How do you utilize the principle of self-discipline in planning and achieving your goals and objectives? Can you give an example of a self-disciplined leader? How do you exercise self-control during times of adversity or crisis?

NOTES: _____
_____
_____
_____
_____
_____
_____
_____
_____
_____
_____

Reflections on Your Leadership Journey

In the space below, record your reflections or thoughts
as you continue your leadership journey:

30.

LEADERS LEAD BY EXAMPLE

◆━━◗ ◖━━◆

"You are Peter, a stone; and upon this rock I will build my church; and all the powers of hell shall not prevail against it."

Matthew 16:18 (TLB)

Since we have such a huge crowd of men of faith watching us from the grandstands, let us strip off anything that slows us down or holds us back, and especially those sins that wrap themselves so tightly around our feet and trip us up; and let us run with patience the particular race that God has set before us. Keep your eyes on Jesus, our leader and instructor.

Hebrews 12:1-2a (TLB)

There are six things the Lord hates—no, seven:
Haughtiness
Lying
Murdering
Plotting evil
Eagerness to do wrong

A false witness
Sowing discord among brothers.

Proverbs 6:16-19 (TLB)

Work hard and become a leader....

Proverbs 12:24a (TLB)

All leaders lead by example. Unfortunately, the example that many leaders exhibit is a bad one.

Effective leaders cannot say, "Do as I say, not do as I do." Such an approach to leadership will ultimately be counterproductive and result in poor leadership examples.

Jesus chose Peter to be the "rock" upon which the new church would be built. Peter was the first disciple to be called by Jesus (Mark 1:16-18) and the first to be named an apostle (Mark 3:14-16). Peter was the recognized leader of the other disciples (Mark 1:36; Luke 22:32). Of course, Peter, as a fallible human being, was not without his faults. However, Peter was the first apostle to see the risen Lord (Luke 24:34; 1 Corinthians 15:5) and he was the first apostle to proclaim salvation to the Gentiles. After Christ was resurrected, Peter set the example as a leader for the other apostles and the members of the early church.

All human beings are imperfect and, thus, are not without their faults. This includes leaders. Therefore, leaders must be viewed in the overall context of their achievements and actions as they lead. Outstanding biblical leaders include: Joseph, Moses, Joshua, Gideon, David, Peter, Barnabas, Pricilla, and Aquilla, just to name a few. Each of these leaders led by example and set the standard for their followers. Being an effective leader isn't easy—it requires hard work (Proverbs 12:24).

James O'Toole, a research professor in the Center for Effective Organizations at the University of Southern California, conducted a study involving several thousand people on four continents. The basis of the study was the question, "Who comes to mind when you hear the words *leader* and *leadership*?"[29] Certain names were most often mentioned, but not a single business leader was listed among the top twenty frequently cited leaders. Likewise, tyrants, such as Hitler, Stalin, Mao, and Castro, were seldom cited as great leaders. Those names most often mentioned included the following (among others):[30]

Mohandas Gandhi
Winston Churchill
Abraham Lincoln
Franklin D. Roosevelt
Martin Luther King, Jr.
Margaret Thatcher
Theodore Roosevelt
Nelson Mandela
Golda Meir
Dwight D. Eisenhower (as a General, not as a President)

What do these leaders have in common? They set a good example for others to follow during times of trial. They were unwavering in their determination to accomplish a specific worthy objective. They could be depended upon to perform "under fire" on behalf of their followers.

Speaking on leadership, Dwight D. Eisenhower said, "A platoon leader [usually a second lieutenant] doesn't get his platoon to go by getting up and shouting and saying, 'I am smarter, I am bigger, I am stronger, I am the leader.' He gets men to go along with him because they want to do it for him [because] they believe in him."[31] Such a leader leads by example—a good example—one that motivates his (or her) men (or women) to follow.

The true nature of leadership has been defined by University of Richmond Professor Joanne Ciculla as follows: "Managers and generals can act like playground bullies and use their power and rank to force their will on people, but this is coercion, not leadership. Leadership is not a person or a position. It is a complex moral relationship between people based on trust, obligation, commitment, emotion and a shared vision of the good."[32]

The Hitlers and other tyrants, although holding ostensible positions of leadership, are examples of the seven things the Lord hates as listed in Proverbs 6:16-19. They represent examples of behavior that leaders should avoid at all costs.

The message in Hebrews 12:1-2 is that we are being watched and judged as leaders. To make sure that we set a good example as a leader, we need to keep our eyes on the standard set by Jesus—who is our *leader* and *instructor*—as we lead through His precepts and example.

APPLICATION: Who do you consider to be a great leader? What type of leadership example do you set for your followers? What can you do to improve your leadership example?

NOTES: _____

_____

_____

_____

_____

_____

_____

_____

_____

31.

LEADERS KNOW THE MEANING OF LOYALTY

Sometime later God tested Abraham. He said to him, "Abraham!" "Here I am," he replied. Then God said, "Take your son, your only son, Isaac, whom you love, and go to the region of Moriah. Sacrifice him there as a burnt offering on one of the mountains I will tell you about."
Genesis 22:1-2 (NIV)

And they answered Joshua, "All that you have commanded us we will do, and wherever you send us we will go. Just as we obeyed Moses in all things, so we will obey you..."
Joshua 1:16-17a (RSV)

Most people will tell you what loyal friends they are, but are they telling the truth?
Proverbs 20:6 (TLB)

"For neither you nor anyone else can serve two masters. You will hate one and show loyalty to the other, or else the other way around—you will be enthusiastic about one and despise the other."
Luke 16:13a (TLB)

"Do as you think best; I'm with you heart and soul, whatever you decide."

1 Samuel 14:7b (TLB)

But Ruth replied, "Don't make me leave you, for I want to go wherever you go, and to live wherever you live; your people shall be my people, and your God shall be my God..."

Ruth 1:16 (TLB)

As a principle of leadership, loyalty must be viewed as a two-way street. If leaders are to expect loyalty from their followers, they must be loyal in return.

There are three levels of loyalty that the Christian leader should practice: loyalty to God, loyalty to superiors, and loyalty to followers. A number of examples of these three types of loyalty are found in the Bible.

Abraham was tested and proved his loyalty to God by his willingness to sacrifice his beloved son, Isaac, the long awaited son of his old age (Genesis 22:1-14). God spared Isaac and provided a substitute sacrifice in the form of a ram caught in a bush.

Joshua's men pledged their loyalty to him as the successor leader to Moses with their response, "All that you have commanded us we will do, and wherever you send us we will go" (Joshua 1:16 RSV). Likewise, Joshua showed loyalty by honoring the promise his men made to Rahab, the prostitute who resided in Jericho. Joshua sent the two men who had spied out the land to rescue Rahab along with her family and arrangements were made for them to live outside the camp of Israel (Joshua 6:22-25).

The principle of loyalty for leaders is not attained through mere lip service. It must be demonstrated by action. General George S. Patton exemplifies this type of loyalty in the command of his troops and in the support of his superiors, even when he didn't always agree with the latter. Alan Axelrod describes such loyalty as follows:

For Patton, loyalty was always a two-way street. For the manager in any situation, loyalty is not some quaint old code of honor, let alone (as some people insist) a macho rite... Loyalty both fuels and lubricates an enterprise.

Contrary to what some managers believe, loyalty is not something simply received from subordinates, like a tax or a tribute. It is always a mutual transaction. You cannot expect loyalty without demonstrating loyalty.

In too many organizations, the prevailing ethic involves a knife in the back. This is, of course, both individually and collectively destructive. Instead, cultivate the sense throughout your organization that, as far as backs are concerned, each member of the group is responsible for watching those of the others. Create loyalty by talking about it and by demonstrating it.[33]

It has been reported that Patton's staff officers were often resentful of what they considered as the unfair treatment accorded General Patton by his immediate superior, General Dwight D. Eisenhower. However, when Patton heard such criticism of Eisenhower, he let his staff know he would not tolerate such talk on their part. He would, of course, argue with Eisenhower in person, but that was a different matter.[34] Patton believed that loyalty to one's superior was an important principle of leadership.

Thus, in the military, as in the case of other organizations as well, loyalty between commanders and the troops serving them must be a two-way street.

Another important biblical lesson concerning loyalty is that "one cannot serve two masters." Our Lord taught that you will hate one and show loyalty to the other, or vice versa (Luke 16:13). Thus, loyalty cannot be divided.

Ruth showed great loyalty to her mother-in-law, Naomi, when she pledged her complete support to Naomi (Ruth 1:16). Such loyalty was the result of both love and respect for Naomi by Ruth. Likewise, Jonathan's armor bearer exhibited great loyalty when he said, "Do as you think best; I'm with you heart and soul, whatever you decide" (1 Samuel 14:7b TLB).

In order for an organization to function effectively, its leaders must know the meaning and importance of loyalty. Leaders must remember that they cannot expect loyalty without demonstrating loyalty. Loyalty is, indeed, a two-way street.

APPLICATION: Why is the practice of loyalty an important leadership principle? Can you give examples of leaders who exemplify the principle of loyalty? How can you implement the meaning and importance of loyalty in your own organization?

NOTES: _____

_____

_____

_____

_____

_____

_____

_____

_____

32.

LEADERS ARE FALLIBLE

◄╍═◑ ◐═╍►

When your people Israel have been defeated by an enemy because they have sinned against you, and when they turn back to you and confess your name, praying and making supplication to you in this temple, then hear from heaven and forgive the sin of your people Israel and bring them back to the land you gave to their fathers.

1 Kings 8:33-34 (NIV)

Your country lies in ruins; your cities are burned; while you watch, foreigners are destroying and plundering everything they see. You stand helpless and abandoned...Listen, you leaders of Israel.... Listen to the Lord. Hear what he is telling you!

Isaiah 1:7-8a; 10b (TLB)

... "Things are not good; the wall of Jerusalem is still torn down, and the gates are burned." ...Then I told them about the desire God had put into my heart, and of my conversation with the king, and the plan to which he had agreed. They replied at once, "Good! Let's rebuild the wall!" And so the work began. ...The wall was finally finished in early September—just fifty-two days after we had begun!

Nehemiah 1:3b; 2:18; 6:15 (TLB)

*Instantly Jesus reached out his hand and rescued [Peter].
"O man of little faith," Jesus said. "Why did you doubt
me?"*

Matthew 14:31 (TLB)

For all have sinned and come short of the glory of God.

Romans 3:23 (KJV)

All leaders are fallible. And all leaders should recognize that the road to success is filled with speed-bumps, potholes, roadblocks, detours, and numerous set-backs in the form of failures, both small and large.

Effective leaders—and especially Christian leaders—should recognize the inevitability of failures and see them as a time for strengthening and renewal. Leaders can use a failure as the beginning of a new opportunity.

If one were to examine the batting average of those baseball players who have achieved admission to the Baseball Hall of Fame, most great hitters have achieved such success with averages far below the perfect standard. In fact, the great baseball legend, Babe Ruth, struck out 1,330 times in order to make 714 home runs. If he had never swung at the ball, he wouldn't have ever struck out—but he wouldn't have made any home runs either.

A key to success as a leader is being able to recognize one's fallibility and to use one's failures as building blocks for later successes. Every failure can be a source of instruction for achieving a future success. Failures can enable the leader to learn from his or her mistakes rather than repeating them to fail again and again. As someone once said, "When life gives you lemons, you need to make lemonade."

Abraham Lincoln was a person who used failures as stepping stones for success. In another chapter, Abraham Lincoln's failures were listed in some detail. Because of these failures—and because Lincoln recognized that he was a fallible human being—Lincoln grew stronger and developed the leadership characteristic of humility, which served to prepare him for the leadership role as President of the United States during the Civil War.

Leaders, as fallible human beings, should recognize that they often have "feet of clay" and "have sinned and come short of the glory of God" (Romans 3:23 KJV). Setbacks and failures can serve to positively reduce the pride that leads to arrogance and the haughtiness which, unless kept in check, will lead to bigger failures (see Proverbs 16:18). A periodic dose of failure can often result in a much needed lesson in humility and thereby serve to make a person a better leader for having suffered it. In the modern vernacular, such might be referred to as an "attitude adjustment."

Ulysses S. Grant is an example of a fallible leader who, in spite of a series of set-backs and failures—including a business failure and being asked to resign his army commission for drunkenness—rose to a level of great success. It would appear that Grant's failures provided him with a strong sense of humility. When Grant met General Robert E. Lee to accept the surrender of the Confederate Army, Lee appeared in a full dress uniform, which was entirely new, and was wearing an ornate sword of considerable value. Conversely, the humble Grant was attired in a standard issue uniform of a lowly army private, with the shoulder straps of a lieutenant general as the only apparent symbol of his position as General-in-Chief of the Union Army.

Christian leaders are not perfect but are forgiven for those sins and transgressions resulting from their fallibility as human beings (of course, not all failure is a result of sin—sometimes we fail simply because we are human). Israel had been defeated by an enemy because they had sinned and had turned their back on God. By praying, making supplication, and asking for forgiveness, they would be able to reverse the situation and get back on the road to success (1 Kings 8:33-34).

Because of poor leadership on the part of their kings, the people of Israel and Judah had turned their backs on God and His commandments. The result was defeat by a foreign enemy and the subsequent exile and deportation of the best and the brightest among the people. While in exile, Nehemiah, who was an able administrator, learned of the desolation of the city of Jerusalem. He knew that without the wall and gates being rebuilt, the city would never be able to return to its former glory since it would continue to be vulnerable to the enemies of the Jews. After receiving permission from Artaxerxes, the king of Persia (Nehemiah was appointed governor of the province), to go and rebuild the wall, he sought God's guidance through prayer. Although Nehemiah encountered numerous setbacks and minor failures—his builders worked with construction tools in one hand and weapons in the other—he, nevertheless, was able to lead the people to success by completing the rebuilding of the wall in fifty-two days.

Samson was a hero of Israel who was known for his great physical strength as well as his fallibilities. During the time of Samson, there was no king in Israel and everyone did what was right in his own eyes (Judges 17:6; 21:25). Samson's life was marred by his weaknesses, including his desire for and involvement with, pagan women, which included a visit to a prostitute in Gaza. Samson was truly a fallible leader. However, after praying to God for strength and redemption, he was able to pull down the pillars of the temple of Dagon (Judges 16:28-31) and win a place among the "heroes of the faith" (Hebrews 11:34).

Moses was fallible. He became angry and killed an Egyptian who was beating a Hebrew slave. Moses made excuses when God directed him to deliver the Israelites out of Egyptian captivity into a "land flowing with milk and honey." Moses' patience reached its breaking point and he sinned against the Lord in anger toward the Hebrew people (Numbers 20:13). However, in spite of his fallibilities, Moses is remembered as an example of a great leader of God's people in time of need (Isaiah 63:12; Micah 6:4; Jeremiah 15:1; Hebrews 11:24-29).

The apostle Peter is another example of a fallible leader. Peter often was impetuous and spoke in haste. He denied Jesus three times after Jesus' arrest. He showed fear and a lack of faith which caused Jesus to rebuke him by saying, "O man of little faith... Why did you doubt me?" (Matthew 14:31 TLB). However, after Jesus' death and resurrection, Peter assumed a key leadership role in the church and is considered as the first Pope by the Roman Catholic Church.

History is replete with stories of fallible leaders. The principle of fallibility is important since leaders need to recognize their mistakes and to use them as positive learning experiences for the accomplishment of future successes. Leaders should accept failure as a *fact* of life, but not as a *way* of life.

Moreover, followers should recognize that their leaders are fallible and that they will never "bat a thousand." Thus, followers should not expect perfection in their leaders but, rather, only expect their leaders to both admit and learn from their mistakes.

APPLICATION: When have you observed fallibility in your leaders? Who can you name who has made mistakes and later was able to achieve success as a leader? How can you use the principle of *Leaders are Fallible* to become a better leader in your own organization?

NOTES: _____

_____

_____

_____

_____

_____

_____

_____

_____

_____

Reflections on Your Leadership Journey

In the space below, record your reflections or thoughts
as you continue your leadership journey:

33.

LEADERS RECOGNIZE AND SEIZE OPPORTUNITIES

◆═◗◖═◆

Jesus called out, "Come along with me and I will show you how to fish for the souls of men!" And they left their nets at once and went with him.

Matthew 4:19-20 (TLB)

"Ask and it will be given to you; seek and you will find; knock and the door will be opened to you."

Matthew 7:7 (NIV)

"As long as it is day, we must do the work of the one who sent me. Night is coming when no one can work."

John 9:4 (NIV)

Jesus replied with this illustration: "A man prepared a great feast and sent out many invitations. When all was ready, he sent his servant around to notify the guests that it was time for them to arrive. But they all began making excuses."

Luke 14:16-18a (TLB)

> *The word of the Lord came to Jonah son of Amittai: "Go to the great city of Nineveh and preach against it..." But Jonah ran away from the Lord and headed to Tarshish. ...Then the Lord came to Jonah a second time: "Go to the great city of Nineveh and proclaim to it the message I give you." Jonah obeyed the word of the Lord and went to Nineveh.*
>
> *Jonah 1:1-3; 3:1-3 (NIV)*

Some eighteen years after Richard M. Nixon resigned the Presidency of the United States, he published a book entitled, *Seize the Moment.* As a student of history and as one who had reflected on the past accomplishments and failures of leaders, Nixon recognized the importance of seizing opportunities.

Successful leaders must be able to both recognize and seize opportunities when they present themselves. Often the window of opportunity is narrow and a decision to act must be made quickly. Unfortunately, too many leaders are prone to procrastination and ignore an opportunity until it is too late and the opportunity no longer exists. Like those who were invited to a banquet feast, they made excuses and did not seize the wonderful opportunity which was made available to them (Luke 14:16-24).

Conversely, others, such as Peter and Andrew, immediately seized upon the opportunity offered to them by Jesus to become "fishers of men" (Matthew 4:18-20 KJV). Peter and Andrew left their nets *at once* and went with Jesus.

If one were to visit a senior citizens' facility, he or she might hear laments such as, "If we had only done *this*, or if we had only done *that*, things would have been different." Such is the lament of lost opportunities. "If only I had invested in IBM stock when it first came out." Or, "If only I had recognized the potential of Microsoft, I would be wealthy today!"

All of us have been blessed with the same twenty-four hours in each day, seven days per week, and 365 days each year. The important question is, how have we used our time? Have we seized the opportunities that God has offered to us? As Jesus reminded His listeners in John 9:4 (NIV), "As long as it is day, we must do the work of the one who sent me. Night is coming when no one can work." *Carpe diem—We must seize the day*!

However, leaders cannot always wait for the opportunity to present itself. Often the leader must take the initiative and the opportunity must be sought out. Once an opportunity is identified, the successful leader moves into action. The prudent leader would do well to seek divine guidance and direction through prayer in determining which opportunity to pursue. As Jesus taught in Matthew 7:7 (NIV), "Ask and it will be given to you; seek and you will find; knock and the door will be opened to you." The leader must take the initiative to *ask*, *seek*, and *knock*. The Scriptures assure us that God will always answer our prayers, although it may not be the answer expected—the answer may be "no," "slow down," or "go!"

During the American Civil War, General George McClellan was known for his reluctance to seize opportunities. His inability to act when the opportunity presented itself proved to be costly in the form of military defeats and, ultimately, the loss of McClellan's opportunity to command the Union Army. Perhaps in no other endeavor is the importance of seizing opportunity as apparent as during times of war. Unlike McClellan, General George S. Patton was a leader who could both recognize and seize opportunities. In his study of the leadership qualities of Patton, Alan Axelrod presents the following observation regarding a leader's ability to recognize opportunity and to seize it:

> *There is a razor-thin line between premature action and seizing opportunity. A good leader recognizes that line.... Whereas ordinary commanders weighed their resources (numbers of men, amount of supplies) against that of the enemy before deciding whether to attack, Patton always added a third element to the equation: time. He recognized that time was a resource as critical as men and supplies and, realizing this, he was often prompted to action even when he possessed less than optimum troop strength. His leadership philosophy was always pragmatic, well suited to*

the imperfect art of war, and, for that matter to an imperfect world: Use what you have when you have to use it. If you wait for perfection, you will lose opportunity.[35]

Fred Smith saw the opportunity for an overnight courier service and founded Federal Express (now known as FedEx®). As Federal Express became a success, others followed and copied Smith's concept. But it was Fred Smith who first recognized and seized the opportunity (despite critics and nay-sayers).

Sometimes an initial failure creates a set-back for the leader. However, often an effective leader can use the failure as an opportunity. Henry Ford said, "Failure is the opportunity to begin again, more intelligently." Jonah failed the first time he was instructed by God to go preach to the people at Nineveh by running away. After his failure, the second time Jonah received instructions he went without hesitation or delay (Jonah 1:1-3; 3:1-3).

Unlike the case of Jonah, a specific opportunity may "knock" only once. Thus, the successful leader must be prepared to recognize and seize an opportunity when it first presents itself.

APPLICATION: What opportunities have you missed because of inaction? What opportunities has the Lord led you to seize? How can you apply the leadership principle of recognizing and seizing opportunities within your own organization?

NOTES: _____
_____
_____
_____
_____
_____
_____
_____

34.

LEADERS ARM THEMSELVES FOR BATTLE

❖⇒◗ ◖⇐❖

So use every piece of God's armor to resist the enemy whenever he attacks, and when it is all over, you will still be standing up. But to do this, you will need the strong belt of truth and the breastplate of God's approval. Wear shoes that are able to speed you on as you preach the Good News of peace with God. In every battle you will need faith as your shield to stop the fiery arrows aimed at you by Satan. And you will need the helmet of salvation and the sword of the Spirit—which is the Word of God.

Ephesians 6:13-17 (TLB)

Every word of God proves true; he is a shield to those who take refuge in him.

Proverbs 30:5 (RSV)

The Lord is my strength and my shield....

Psalms 28:7a (KJV)

I n an earlier chapter, leaders were reminded of the saying, "When you soar like an eagle you attract hunters."

As leaders, we can expect to be under constant attack by those who want to see us fail and by Satan who wants all Christian leaders to fail. Thus, leaders must be vigilant and prepare for the inevitable battles which come to all those who lead.

Paul writes about the need to prepare for battle in his letter to the church at Ephesus (Ephesians 6:10-18). During the writing of Ephesians, Paul was a prisoner of the Romans and was guarded by soldiers in four-hour shifts. As Paul observed the armed soldiers, he was reminded that Christians should arm themselves with God's armor in anticipation of the battles which ultimately will be fought.[36]

Thus, it is not a question of *if* the battles will come; but, rather, it is only a question of *when*. Therefore, it would behoove successful leaders to be prepared and armed for battle.

Paul tells us to first put on the "belt of truth." A solider during Paul's time would gather up his long robe or tunic and secure it with a girdle or belt. This was done in preparation for battle. Such preparation has been referred to in the Bible as "girding up your loins." Along with such physical preparedness is the mental preparation that the leader must do prior to engaging the enemy. Paul refers to this mental preparation elsewhere with the analogy of "girding up the loins of your mind," i.e., having a proper mental attitude.

The word "truth" is used in reference to the "belt." Leaders should remember that the truth is our friend, our strength, and our weapon. The enemy seeks to spread lies and distortions about the Christian leader in an attempt to discredit him or her. Leaders should know the truth that comes from the Word of God and thereby live truthfully and with integrity.

The opposite of truth is a lie. Those who lie are required to tell another lie in order to cover up the lie they previously told. Leaders must avoid lies, walk in the truth, and remember that Satan is the "father of lies."

The next piece of armor is the "breastplate of righteousness" (Ephesians 6:14 KJV). The breastplate protected the soldier from the neck to his waist. This piece of armor symbolizes God's approval of the leader's actions. Thus, the leader must make sure that his or her position is one that would be approved by God based upon the circumstances and the guidance provided by the Holy Scriptures. Such brings to mind the single most important question a leader should ask before making a major decision: "What would Jesus do?"

Next, the leader is to put on the "shoes of the Gospel of Peace." Roman soldiers are said to have worn special, hobnailed sandals, thereby enabling them to remain strong and unwavering in their stand. The Gospel of Peace refers to the peace that Christ achieved through his reconciliation of man with God through Jesus' death on the cross. The knowledge of this peace, through reconciliation, allows us to stand firm in our reliance on the Lord and the power of His might (Ephesians 6:10).

Leaders are to use the "shield of faith" as they prepare for battle. The ancient Romans had special shields which could be locked together thereby allowing them to move forward against the enemy as a single unit. These shields deflected the "fiery arrows" which were assailed against them by the enemy. Leaders can expect to be assailed by the "fiery arrows" of those who wish to see them fail. Such arrows include lies, deceit, ugly thoughts, pride, envy, and false and malicious rumors. Leaders should look to the Lord as their shield as has been described in the Scriptures: "Every word of God is pure, he is a shield to those who put their trust in Him" (Proverbs 30:5 KJV) and "The Lord is my strength and my shield" (Psalm 28:7 KJV).

The "helmet of salvation" is to be used to protect the leader's mind so that he or she has the necessary confidence and positive mental attitude required to fight the day-to-day battles which all leaders must face. We have the truth of who we are in Christ and that Christ has paid the price for our salvation. As fallible humans, we need to be reminded of this fact since the enemy will attempt to demoralize us and seek to attack those areas in which we are particularly vulnerable. Leaders need to protect their minds from corruption of those things in the world that might adversely influence us and cause us to make the wrong leadership decisions.

Up to this point, all of the armor described by Paul has been of a defensive nature, i.e., used to protect the Christian leader from attack. However, the last piece of armor is an offensive weapon—the sword of the Spirit, which is the Word of God. The Bible provides the arsenal where the leader's swords are located. The sword of the Spirit is that specific Word of God which is needed for a particular occasion or circumstance. When Jesus was tempted by Satan in the wilderness, he used specific Scriptures to fight against, and to disarm, Satan (Matthew 4:1-10). And, after Jesus quoted the Scriptures, Satan left him. One offensive action that the leader can take is to determine his or her area of vulnerability and commit to memory those specific Scriptures which can be used as "swords" to disarm the enemy when he attacks.

Without the whole armor of God, a leader remains vulnerable and stands to lose his or her battles. Leaders should remember, "Greater is he that is in you, than he that is in the world" (1 John 4:4 KJV). Thus, leaders can be victorious over the enemy in the name of Jesus Christ.

The battles which leaders will face are inevitable. "Your enemy the devil prowls around like a roaring lion looking for someone to devour" (1 Peter 5:8 NIV). Therefore, successful leaders must always be armed and ready for battle. And, the whole armor of God is the proper equipment leaders need to be victorious in the pursuit of their worthy goals and objectives.

APPLICATION: When have you been vulnerable as a leader? When have you been attacked through the use of lies, innuendos, or false rumors? When have you used the whole armor of God to protect you and enable you to achieve victory?

NOTES: _____

_____

_____

_____

_____

_____

35.

LEADERS SEEK WISE COUNSEL

Then Absalom turned to Ahithophel and asked him, "What shall I do next?" Ahithophel told him, "Go and sleep with your father's wives, for he has left them here to keep the house. Then all Israel will know that you have insulted him beyond the possibility of reconciliation, and they will all close ranks behind you."

2 Samuel 16:20-21 (TLB)

The godly man is a good counselor because he is just and fair and knows right from wrong.

Psalms 37:30-31 (TLB)

Listen to advice and accept instruction, that you may gain wisdom for the future.

Proverbs 19:20 (RSV)

Make plans by seeking advice; if you wage war, obtain guidance.

Proverbs 20:18 (NIV)

Plans go wrong with too few counselors; many counselors bring success.

Proverbs 15:22 (TLB)

Give instruction to a wise man, and he will be still wiser.

Proverbs 9:9a (RSV)

Without wise leadership, a nation is in trouble; but with good counselors there is safety.

Proverbs 11:14 (TLB)

A leader cannot be expected to be an expert in all subjects. Therefore, leaders must of necessity seek and accept wise counsel from others who are qualified to provide sound advice.

As this chapter is being written, America is in the throes of a heated political campaign for the presidency of the United States (along with other elected offices). No one person can know all of the answers to the problems which may face a nation—the economy, threats of terrorism, war, crime, poverty, international relations, and domestic issues. The position of President of the United States, perhaps more than any other leadership position, brings to mind the importance of seeking wise counsel.

The leaders of large corporations cannot know how to perform in every position of importance. Thus, they hire persons who are competent to fill those positions which are instrumental to the success and failure of the organization. They look to a board of directors to further guide them in their major decisions. They hire outside consultants and advisors to provide further wise counsel before embarking on new ventures or major undertakings.

Some leaders from large corporations are currently facing criminal prosecution for the acts of those who were chosen to lead and manage various important divisions of those corporations. A defense presented by some of these CEOs is that they "didn't know what their subordinates were doing." And, in many cases, they probably didn't know, especially within those organizations consisting of thousands of employees and multi-national offices.

Such circumstances emphasize the importance of leaders seeking and receiving wise counsel from capable and trusted advisors. History is replete with examples of those who received bad advice, although at the time they believed such counsel was good and appropriate. In another chapter, the example was given of Sears Roebuck and Montgomery Ward, both of which were about the same size following World War II. The leader of Sears, General Wood, chose expansion while Sewell Avery, the leader of Montgomery Ward, chose to wait for what was believed to be another economic depression. Both received what each believed to be wise counsel from their advisors. However, history proved Sears' choice to be correct and Montgomery Ward's course of action to be wrong.

Most organizations today are operated with a board of directors, or trustees, who are there to provide wise counsel rather than a "rubber stamp" on the decisions of one or two individuals. And, while such directors must select competent leaders carefully, those leaders must be men or women who will both seek and accept wise counsel when it is provided.

Absalom, the son of King David, attempted to overthrow his father and become the King of Israel. One of Absalom's advisors was Ahithophel, who advised him to engage in despicable behavior regarding King David's wives (2 Samuel 16:20-23). Ahithophel had previously been an advisor to King David and, perhaps, was one of the reasons Absalom so readily followed his advice. The Scriptures provide the following account: "Absalom did whatever Ahithophel told him to, just as David had; for every word Ahithophel spoke was as wise as though it had come directly from the mouth of God" (2 Samuel 16:23 TLB). Ahithophel's counsel was, in fact, unwise and an abomination to the laws of both God and men. Ahithophel's advise to Absalom directly contributed to his defeat and death.

Leaders must function within the framework of both organizations and society in order to accomplish worthy goals and objectives. To do so, they must seek and accept the wise counsel of godly persons who are expert in their particular fields of discipline. "The godly man is a good counselor because he is just and fair and knows right from wrong" (Psalms 37:30-31 TLB). Likewise, the successful leader should seek advice from several advisors, prayerfully consider the advice given, and then make the final decision. "Plans go wrong with too few counselors; many counselors bring success" (Proverbs 15:22 TLB).

While the final decision may ultimately remain with the leader who is in charge, his or her seeking of wise counsel will serve to assure that the best possible decision has been made based upon the facts and circumstances at hand.

APPLICATION: Why is wise counsel so important to leaders? Name several prominent leaders who, in your opinion, achieved success because they sought and accepted wise counsel. How can you use the wise counsel of others to lead your own organization more successfully?

NOTES: _____

_____

_____

_____

_____

_____

_____

_____

_____

36.

LEADERS PURSUE WISDOM

◇═◐ ◑═◇

The Lord was pleased with [Solomon's] reply and was glad that Solomon asked for wisdom. So [the Lord] replied, "Because you have asked for wisdom in governing my people...yes, I'll give you what you have asked for! I will give you a wiser mind than anyone else has ever had or ever will have!"

1 Kings 3:10-12 (TLB)

And God gave Solomon wisdom and understanding beyond measure, and a largeness of mind like the sand on the seashore...

1 Kings 4:29 (RSV)

Happy is the man who finds wisdom and the man who gets understanding, for the gain from it is better than gain from silver and its profit better than gold.

Proverbs 3:13-14 (RSV)

Wisdom has been defined as *knowledge and good judgment based on experience.* This leads us to the next logical question: Just how do we go about attaining such wisdom?

Solomon could have asked God for many things including riches, fame, honor, and a long life. Rather than these, he asked God for "an understanding mind so that I can govern your people well and know the difference between what is right and what is wrong" (1 Kings 3:9 TLB). This request was preceded by Solomon's admission that he was, in fact, poorly equipped for the job given to him—that of king of Israel. Solomon was assuming the throne previously held by the great King David. Thus, Solomon confessed, "O Lord my God, now you have made me the king instead of my father, David, but I am as a little child who doesn't know his way around" (1 Kings 3:7 TLB).

By our viewing Solomon as an example, perhaps our first step toward gaining wisdom is the acknowledgement of how little we really know. Thus, the aspiring leader must consider the following two-part question: How and where does one obtain wisdom?

It would appear that the answer to this question lies in the definition of wisdom stated above. We receive wisdom through *knowledge* and *experience*. Both of these ingredients—knowledge and experience—are necessary if we are to exercise good judgment as leaders.

In today's modern society, we generally gain knowledge through formal education. But education alone does not make us wise. Who wants to be the first client of a lawyer who just graduated from law school? Who wants to be the first patient of a physician who just graduated from medical school? In these two examples, the lawyer is the most dangerous since he or she needs absolutely no experience to practice law. Rather, the only requirement is a license which is the result of having passed an examination. A least the doctor, in comparison, is required to complete a minimum of one year of internship or residency before he or she can be granted a license in most jurisdictions.

Frequently, the young college graduate is thrust into a position of leadership and authority with little or no actual preparation for such a position. The actual experience that follows is often painful.

In the Living Bible, 1 Kings 4:29 is translated as, "God gave Solomon great wisdom and understanding and a mind with broad interests." One might conclude that Solomon's broad interests provided him with a knowledge of many subjects which further served to enhance his wisdom. We are told that he was the author of 3,000 proverbs and wrote 1,005 songs. The Scriptures record that he was a great naturalist, with an interest in animals, birds, snakes, fish, and trees (1 Kings 4:32-33).

Those leaders who were the founders of the United States of America were men of great wisdom and broad interests. Although a lawyer by profession, Thomas Jefferson had some 8,000 books covering a wide variety of subjects in his personal library. It has been reported that Jefferson had read each of these books at least four times. Jefferson's knowledge of the Holy Scriptures was an influence in his drafting of the Declaration of Independence which included the following words: "...that all men are created equal, that they are endowed by their Creator with certain unalienable Rights, that among these are Life, Liberty and the pursuit of Happiness." During his second term as President, Jefferson offered a national prayer which included a request for wisdom for this nation's leaders: "Almighty God, Who has given us this good land for our heritage...Endow with Thy spirit of wisdom those to whom in Thy Name we entrust the authority of government ...." [37]

As Christian leaders, we have a responsibility to expand and stretch our minds through the study of a variety of subjects which extend beyond our vocations or professions. Such study should, of necessity, include the regular reading of God's Word through structured Bible studies. For those leaders who have not already done so, it is recommended that a program be implemented to read the Bible through in its entirety—from Genesis through Revelation—over a period of 12 months.

Our knowledge of the Holy Scriptures will serve to provide us with a *moral compass* which can and will assist us in our leadership decision-making.

As Christian leaders, we also need to turn to prayer and ask God to grant us wisdom as we are faced with difficult and important leadership decisions.

The Book of Proverbs is referred to as one of the "Wisdom Books" of the Bible. Its instructions can provide valuable insight for the aspiring as well as the seasoned leader. And since there are 31 chapters in Proverbs, it is recommended that one chapter be read every day of the month throughout the year. References to "wisdom" appear some 54 times in the Book of Proverbs.

Since leadership development is a never-ending journey, leaders are encouraged to continue the pursuit of wisdom through additional education and experience throughout their careers. As it is written in proverbs, "Wisdom is the tree of life to those who eat her fruit; happy is the man who keeps on eating it" (Proverbs 3:18 TLB).

APPLICATION: Name two or more modern leaders who you believe possess a high degree of wisdom. What role do you think wisdom plays in the leadership of a successful organization? How will you be able to acquire wisdom for your own personal growth?

NOTES: _____

_____

_____

_____

_____

_____

_____

_____

_____

37.

LEADERS CAN
SUCCEED WITH SUCCESS

King Solomon married many other girls besides the Egyptian princess. Many of them came from nations where idols were worshiped...even though the Lord had clearly instructed his people not to marry into those nations.... Yet Solomon did it anyway.

1 Kings 11:1-2 (TLB)

Blessed is the man who walks not in the counsel of the wicked...He is like a tree planted by streams of water, that yields its fruit in its season, and its leaf does not wither. In all that he does, he prospers.

Psalms 1:1-3 (RSV)

Commit your work to the Lord, then it will succeed.

Proverbs 16:3 (TLB)

Pride ends in destruction; humility ends in honor.

Proverbs 18:12 (TLB)

We can justify our every deed but God looks at our motives.

Proverbs 21:2 (TLB)

Don't praise yourself; let others do it!
                                                    Proverbs 27:2 (TLB)

Here is my final conclusion: fear God and obey his commandments, for this is the entire duty of man. For God will judge us for everything we do, including every hidden thing, good or bad.
                                            Ecclesiastes 12:13-14 (TLB)

Jesus called them together and said, "You know that the rulers of the Gentiles lord it over them, and their high officials exercise authority over them. Not so with you. Instead, whoever wants to become great among you must be your servant..."
                                              Matthew 20:25-26 (NIV)

In 1957, a motion picture was released with the title, "Will Success Spoil Rock Hunter?" It starred Tony Randall and Jayne Mansfield and was intended to be a satire of the advertising business. The theme song for this movie was "You've Got It Made!"

This particular motion picture should make the leader mindful that success brings with it certain pitfalls. And, if the successful leader is not careful, his or her success may well lead to eventual disaster. Thus, the question is: *How can leaders succeed with success?*

Success has a tendency to "spoil" the leader, i.e., to create a sense of false pride and arrogance, and to cause the leader to lose sight of those very qualities which contributed to his or her success during an earlier time in his or her career. There are numerous leadership lessons in the Bible which can help leaders to succeed with success, not the least of which involve some of the greatest leaders of Israel—David and Solomon.

David, the greatest king in the history of Israel, allowed his success and the blessings of God to be "spoiled" when he took Bathsheba in an act of adultery and, thereafter, provided instructions which resulted in the death of her husband, Uriah the Hittite.

Likewise, David's son, King Solomon, who was said to be the wisest man on earth, succumbed to failings in his later years by marrying foreign women and allowing them to worship pagan idols in open violation of God's commandments.

Perhaps one of the worst dangers that successful leaders can encounter is the destructive power of the pride that accompanies one's success. Successful leaders too often begin to believe their own "press releases" and lose the God-given attribute of humility (see Proverbs 27:2). They begin to believe that they are allowed to have a different set of standards and that the accepted rules of conduct are applicable only to others and not to them. Success has the ability to blind a leader and to ultimately result in his or her fall. Napoleon, who thought he and his army were invincible, found defeat at a place called Waterloo. Although the British general, Charles Cornwallis, was convinced of his superiority over the poorly trained Continental Army of George Washington, he led the fateful Carolina Campaign and was ultimately defeated at Yorktown. While early successes convinced Adolph Hitler that he could eventually conquer the entire world, his prediction of a thousand-year Reich lasted only twelve years.

Thus, success in business, government, or in any field of endeavor can frequently create a level of pride and haughtiness that will cause the leader to make reckless decisions. Such leaders often lose sight of humility and those positive qualities of leadership which propelled them to success in the first place. "Pride ends in destruction; humility ends in honor" (Proverbs 18:12 TLB).

It would appear that any person who has achieved the highest office in this nation—President of the United States—has reached the ultimate pinnacle of success as a leader. However, the White House, itself, has been described as a "character crucible." In the book, *A Matter of Character*, Ronald Kessler presents the following observation about the presidency:

> *No one can imagine the kind of pressure that being president of the United States imposes on an individual and how easily a president can be corrupted by power....*
>
> *"Here is where true strength of character of the person,*

not his past accomplishments, will determine whether his presidency ends in accomplishment or failure."

...Thus, unless a president comes to office with good character and competence, the crushing force of the office and the adulation the chief executive receives will inevitably lead to disaster.[38]

To succeed with success, leaders must keep in mind the importance of "servanthood." The organization is not created for the leader—rather, the leader is there for the organization and its worthy mission. This was an important lesson which Jesus taught to his disciples: "Jesus called them together and said, 'You know that the rulers of the Gentiles lord it over them, and their high officials exercise authority over them. Not so with you. Instead, whoever wants to become great among you must be your servant...'" (Matthew 20:25-26 NIV) This teaching immediately followed the request from the mother of two of his disciples, James and John, for Jesus to command that her two sons be placed one on the right hand of Jesus and the other on His left.

The successful leader must commit his or her work to worthwhile goals and objectives and not deviate from the straight and narrow path. Conversely, wrong objectives, or motives, chart a course for disaster. As Proverbs states, "We can justify our every deed but God looks at our motives" (Proverbs 21:2 TLB).

A leader who becomes successful must always remember *what is right* and *what is his or her duty* as a leader. "For God will judge us for everything we do, including every hidden thing, good or bad" (Ecclesiastes 12:13-14 TLB). A leader who can succeed with success will be as the psalmist described, "...like a tree planted by streams of water, that yields its fruit in its season, and its leaf does not wither. In all that he does, he prospers" (Psalms 1:1-3 RSV).

How can leaders succeed with success? Fervent prayer and a solid grounding in the Word of God, when combined with wise counsel from godly men and women, will serve to enable leaders to succeed with success.

APPLICATION: Why are many apparently successful leaders unable to succeed with success? What are some of the pitfalls that lie in the pathway of successful leaders? What can you do to assure that you will be able to succeed with success?

NOTES: _____

_____

_____

_____

_____

_____

_____

_____

_____

_____

Reflections on Your Leadership Journey

In the space below, record your reflections or thoughts
as you continue your leadership journey:

38.

LEADERS ARE A WORK IN PROGRESS

⤙⟹⟸⤚

A man who refuses to admit his mistakes can never be successful. But if he confesses and forsakes them, he gets another chance.

Proverbs 28:13 (TLB)

And be renewed in the spirit of your mind; And that ye put on the new man, which after God is created in righteousness and true holiness.

Ephesians 4:23-24 (KJV)

...what counts is whether we really have been changed into new and different people.

Galatians 6:15b (TLB)

Becoming a successful leader is not merely a destination; rather, it is a journey. It involves continuous development and a reshaping of the person over the life and career of the leader—*it requires that the leader be a work in progress!*

This process was recognized by the great American clergyman,

Harry Emerson Fosdick, who described personal development in the following manner: "[It] is not so much like a structure as like a river [which] continually flows, and to be a person is to be engaged in a perpetual process of becoming." Thus, the successful leader must realize that he or she, too, is in a *perpetual process of becoming.*

All of a leader's experiences, good or bad, serve to shape us into the persons we ultimately become (see chapters on Synergism and Wilderness Experience). It is often the more serious trials and tribulations which have the greatest and most positive effect on the leader's personal development. As Johan Wolfgang von Goethe said, "Talents are best nurtured in solitude [but] character is best formed in the stormy billows of the world."

Being a leader means that one must continually "reinvent" himself or herself as he or she continues on life's journey as a leader. Such reinventing, or development, comes about through a planned and structured process of leadership development. It often takes the form of formal academic courses, Bible studies, reading lists, or in-service training of various types. Physicians are required to participate in "continuing medical education" programs and lawyers are required to take "continuing legal education" courses as prerequisites for maintaining a professional license. Such requirements often also apply to teachers, accountants, and licensed real estate agents, among others. All of these continuing education requirements are based on the premise that one must grow and not become stagnant—that one must continue to "stay up" with the latest developments in a particular profession or vocation. (It is hoped that this book, *Leadership Lessons From the Bible*, will serve as a resource for continuing leadership development.)

The leadership principle of *a work in progress* can be viewed in the lives of numerous leaders in the Bible, in both the Old and New Testaments. Joseph of the Old Testament is a good example of a work in progress. From a spoiled brat and later a slave, he became a great leader who was second only to the Egyptian Pharaoh. Through all of his experiences, Joseph continued to grow as a person and as a leader. Likewise, the disciple Peter developed from a hot-tempered fisherman into the recognized and highly effective leader of the early Christian church. Jesus recognized Peter's potential when he was chosen and Peter continued to grow and develop as "a work in progress."

Some years ago, the author suggested that a teaching colleague read a newly published book relating to business administration. This particular colleague held a graduate degree in business administration from a prestigious university. However, his reaction to this offer was both startling and unexpected. He responded, "I haven't read a business book since I received my M.B.A. and I'm not going to start now!" Such an attitude, although hopefully uncommon, leads to complacency and stagnation on the part of any person but, in particular, those who are placed in positions of leadership.

Being a Christian, in itself, requires continuous development and growth. As the apostle Paul indicated, we become a new creation and strive to grow in the likeness of Jesus Christ. As Christians we continue to seek a level of perfection we know we will never achieve in our lifetime because we are fallible human beings—but, regardless, we continue to strive toward this goal. In this way, we become new persons who are, though our acceptance of Jesus Christ, a work in progress (see Ephesians 4:17-24).

Successful leaders also recognize their mistakes and are willing to learn from such mistakes. The recognition and admission of mistakes are part of the leader's growth and development (Proverbs 28:13).

Modern psychologists, such as Abraham Maslow and Fredrick W. Hertzberg, have presented theories regarding the motivation and progression of human beings. Both Maslow and Hertzberg viewed life as a continuing quest for the achievement of goals and objectives which, in fact, may never be realized. In leadership, these goals are never met because the successful leader, like the successful athlete, continually "raises the bar" so that his or her goals become harder to achieve when new standards replace old ones.

Great leaders never achieve their ultimate goals during their lifetimes. Why? Because they recognize that they are *a work in progress* and, as such, are in a *perpetual process of becoming.*

APPLICATION: What leaders can you name who exemplify the concept of "a work in progress?" Why is it important that we, as leaders, acknowledge that we are "a work in progress?" How will you apply the principle of "a work in progress" to your own growth and development as a leader?

NOTES: _____

_____

_____

_____

_____

_____

_____

_____

_____

_____

39.

LEADERS PREPARE FOR PASSING THE MANTLE OF AUTHORITY

[The Lord spoke to Elijah saying] "you shall anoint [Elisha] to be prophet in your place." ...So he departed from there, and found Elisha the son of Shaphat, who was plowing, with twelve yoke of oxen before him, and he was with the twelfth. Elijah passed by him and cast his mantle upon him.

1 Kings 19:16c, 19 (RSV)

When David's time to die drew near, he charged Solomon his son saying, "I am about to go the way of all the earth. Be strong and show yourself a man, and keep the charge of the Lord your God, walking in his ways and keeping his statutes, his commandments, his ordinances, and his testimonies, as it is written in the law of Moses, that you may prosper in all that you do and wherever you turn...." So Solomon sat upon the throne of David his father; and his kingdom was firmly established.

1 Kings 2:1-3; 12 (RSV)

After the death of Moses, the Lord's disciple, God spoke to Moses' assistant, whose name was Joshua (the son of Nun), and said to him, "Now that my disciple is dead, [you are the new leader of Israel]. Lead my people across the Jordan River into the Promised Land."

Joshua 1:1-2 (TLB)

Effective leaders know that eventually the time will come for them to pass the "mantle of authority" to a successor.

Two situations usually create a need to choose a successor. The first is when the leader is promoted to a higher position of authority. Here, there must be a successor to assume those duties previously performed by the promoted leader. The second situation is one in which a leader reaches that stage of his or her life when retirement or death creates the need for a successor.

Joshua was Moses' successor and a man who led the nation of Israel across the Jordan River and into the Promised Land. He also led the Israelites as they conquered and settled the land.

Joshua was well prepared to receive the mantle of authority previously held by Moses. In the Wilderness of Sinai, Moses took his assistant, Joshua, with him when he went up the mountain to talk to God (Exodus 24:13). Moses gave Joshua a prominent place at the Tabernacle. Joshua was selected by Moses as one of the twelve spies sent to scout out the land of Canaan. After assuming the leadership of the Hebrews, Joshua supervised the division of the territory among the twelve tribes and led the people to renew their covenant with God. As Moses' successor, Joshua was well prepared to complete the work that Moses had begun.

While the preparation of Solomon was not extensive, David apparently saw in him those characteristics which would make Solomon an effective leader. David also had promised Bathsheba that Solomon would be his successor, to lead in a specific way in keeping with God's commandments and the law of Moses.

At the direction of God, Elijah found Elisha plowing with a team of oxen and Elijah threw his mantle over the younger man. Elisha followed Elijah and became his servant (1 Kings 19:21).

Before Elijah ascended to heaven in a chariot of fire, he fulfilled Elisha's final request by providing him with a double portion of his prophetic spirit (2 Kings 2:9-10). After receiving Elijah's mantle of authority, Elisha parted the waters of the Jordan River enabling him to walk across dry ground (2 Kings 2:14) as a demonstration that he had received God's blessing as Elijah's successor.

Leaders are frequently remiss in preparing their successors to assume the mantle of authority. Although in ill health for some time, President Franklin Roosevelt had not prepared his Vice President, Harry S. Truman, for the responsibilities of the presidency. After Roosevelt's untimely death, the new President found out that he had been kept in the dark about numerous matters within the government including the Manhattan Project—the development of the atomic bomb by the Roosevelt administration. While the atomic bomb was certainly a matter of utmost secrecy, surely the Vice President should have been apprised of this project as well as other important matters of government. Historians now believe that President Roosevelt's poor health created a situation whereby he was ill-equipped to negotiate effectively, when he met with the Russian leader, Joseph Stalin, at Yalta in February, 1945.

Peter was the leader of the early church in Jerusalem. However, after his miraculous release from prison (see Acts 12), it appears that he left Jerusalem for "another place." The mantle of leadership of the Jerusalem church was passed from Peter to James, the brother of Jesus. Although we see Peter participating in the Council of Jerusalem (Acts 15:12-21), James assumed the mantle of authority and considered it his calling to oversee the church in Jerusalem. Together, James, Peter, and John were considered to be the "pillars" of the church (Galatians 2:9). It has been said that, after passing the mantle of leadership of the Jerusalem church to James, Peter probably broadened his ministry of the Gospel and became a more effective leader.

In particular, church pastors, who have been responsible for the growth and success of a specific church, are reluctant to recognize that their effectiveness has begun to wane. They often refuse to choose a successor or even consider retirement. Like many of us, they believe that *no one* can replace them.

As this is being written, Michael Eisner, the C.E.O. of the Walt Disney Company for the past 20 years, is under fire by large outside investors and his board of directors. One criticism of Eisner has been that he has refused to choose and groom an able successor. He had been quoted as saying that he intends to "die in this job."

As leaders, we have a responsibility to prepare others to assume the mantle of authority when we can no longer serve effectively. To do so, we must be realistic and implement such preparations even when it is our human nature to think we can do the job better than anyone else and that we will be able to serve beyond our reasonable time. Leaders need to remember that no person is indispensable.

One school of management thought contends that a leader should "know when to leave." George Washington probably could have been elected to a third term as President, but he knew when it was time to leave. In like manner, a leader needs to know when he or she should prepare to pass the mantle of authority to a successor.

APPLICATION: Can you name a modern leader who has passed his or her level of effectiveness but has refused to pass the mantle of leadership to a successor? How should we go about preparing a successor? Are you preparing a successor in order to allow you to be promoted or to move on to other areas of growth and development?

NOTES: _____

_____

_____

_____

_____

_____

_____

_____

_____

40.

LEADERS RECOGNIZE GOD AS THE CENTER OF THEIR LEADERSHIP

If you want favor with God and man, and a reputation for good judgment and common sense, then trust the Lord completely... In everything you do, put God first and he will direct and crown your efforts with success.

Proverbs 3:4-6 (TLB)

"From the time I brought your forefathers up from Egypt until today, I warned them again and again, saying, 'Obey me.'"

Jeremiah 11:7 (NIV)

... "When one rules over men in righteousness, when he rules in the fear of God, he is like the light of morning at sunrise on a cloudless morning..."

2 Samuel 23:3b-4a (NIV)

"At the end of seven years I, Nebuchadnezzar, looked up to heaven, and my sanity returned, and I praised and

*worshiped the Most High God and honored him who lives
forever, whose rule is everlasting, his kingdom ever-
more.... No one can stop him or challenge him..."*
Daniel 4:34-35b (TLB)

To be successful, leaders must recognize that their ultimate success flows from God. Thus, it is God alone who must be recognized as the source of their success and as the center of their leadership.

As previous chapters have illustrated, when leaders forget the place of God in their leadership endeavors, they will fail. God's standards, as set forth in his Holy Scriptures, should be the leader's guide in all that he or she does.

One of the greatest dangers that leaders can encounter is the belief that their success was attained solely by their own efforts. Leaders must rely on a "higher power"—the power that comes from God as the center of their leadership.

Those biblical leaders who recognized this principle of leadership achieved lasting success. These include Abraham, Joseph, Moses, Joshua, Gideon, Peter, and Paul, just to name a few. Others, who failed to recognize God as the center of their leadership, saw their success as only temporary since it was based on leadership without the inclusion and blessings of God.

King Nebuchadnezzar of Babylon is an example of a leader who ignored God and viewed all accomplishments as being the result of his efforts alone. When Nebuchadnezzar made an arrogant boast about all that he had achieved (Daniel 4:30), he was stricken at the height of his power and pride by God's judgment. He was driven out of his leadership position and made to live with the beasts of the field. His hair grew like the feathers of an eagle and his nails were like birds' claws. This condition lasted for seven years. However, there was a happier ending for Nebuchadnezzar. He repented and recognized that God, not man, was responsible for a ruler's success. Then he blessed God and praised and honored and glorified Him. Nebuchadnezzar then acknowledged, "[God's] dominion is an eternal dominion; his kingdom endures from generation to generation...No one can hold back [God's] hand...." (Daniel 4:34b-35 NIV).

After Nebuchadnezzar's repentance, his honor, glory, and kingdom were restored along with his counselors and officers, and he was reestablished as the leader of his kingdom (Daniel 4:36-37a). This story ends with the following realization by Nebuchadnezzar: "...those who walk in pride [God] is able to humble" (Daniel 4:37b NIV).

Historically, corrupt nations and/or organizations have never prevailed. Rather, their successes have been only temporary, resulting in eventual failure. Conversely, those leaders who placed their faith and trust in God have enabled their nations and organizations to endure.

The United States of America is an example of a nation that has recognized God as the center of its leadership. God has blessed the United States since its founding. Its leaders, although fallible, have continued over these past 200 years to acknowledge God's role in their leadership and His dominion over this nation—a nation under God. Thomas Paine said: "The cause of America is in a great measure the cause of all mankind.... The Almighty implanted in us these inextinguishable feelings for good and wise purposes. They are the guardians of His image in our heart..."[39]

Our leaders' recognition and reliance on the guidance of the Almighty is evident. Many of our public buildings have been adorned with either biblical quotations or references to God. God's Ten Commandments are the very foundation of our body of laws. Our currency states, "In God we trust."

It was reported that President George W. Bush hung an oil painting in the Oval Office—the same one he had hung in the Texas Governor's Mansion—entitled *A Charge to Keep*, which was based on a popular hymn written by Charles Wesley, a founder of the Methodist Church. When asked about the message of the hymn, the President responded, "We serve One greater than ourselves."[40]

On March 4, 1805, Thomas Jefferson, in his Second Inaugural Address, stated:

I shall now enter on the duties to which my fellow-citizens have again called me....

I shall need, too, the favor of that Being in whose hands we are, who led our forefathers, as Israel of old, from their native land and planted them in a country flowing with all the necessities and comforts of life, who has covered our infancy with His Providence and our riper years with His wisdom and power, and to whose goodness I ask you to join with me in supplications that He will so enlighten the minds of your servants, guide their councils and prosper their measures ....[41]

Now, as then, leaders of all nations of the world, but in particular those of the United States of America—from the lowest level supervisor to the highest leader in government—need to recognize that God is the center of their leadership. With such recognition and reliance, our leaders will continue to prosper and achieve success for themselves, their organizations, and this great nation.

APPLICATION: Why should God be placed at the center of our leadership? What leaders can you name who have recognized this ultimate principle of leadership? How can you become a better leader by making God the center of your leadership?

NOTES: _____

_____

_____

_____

_____

_____

_____

_____

_____

EPILOGUE

O ver a period spanning some four decades, I have either experienced or observed—while in leadership positions involving the military, education, business, the legal field, and the church—all of the 40 leadership principles included in this book.

Along the way I have encountered pitfalls and struggles, stumbled and fallen, stumbled and fallen again, and lived through a wilderness experience. Some of my experiences and observations included the "good, the bad, and the ugly." However, all have enabled me to view the subject of leadership from a real-world perspective.

Since this book was first begun, I have become more acutely aware of the leadership crisis that is facing America at all levels and in all organizational endeavors.

Yes, we have leaders—men and women with titles—who have been charged with the responsibility of leading departments, companies, churches, non-profit entities, the armed forces and our governments, from the city and county level to the nation's capitol. But, how effective are they?

Corporate scandals, along with poor leadership in the military, have given us WorldCom, Enron, and Abu Ghraib. Headlines, editorials, and feature articles continue to blurt out the words "poor leadership" as an almost endemic cause of these problems. The simple question is "Why?"

One former military commander viewed the solution to the leadership problem as one of simply assuring that honorable and decent men and women are chosen to lead. This was based on a view that those who follow appear to fit into several categories: that small percentage (perhaps ten percent) who will always do their duty regardless of the competence of their leaders or the obstacles placed in their way; a like percentage who will never do their duty regardless of who is chosen to lead; and the remainder, who will perform either as heroes or as a self-centered, undisciplined mob depending upon who is leading them.

Thus, the one who leads must possess something more than a college diploma or the training found in corporate America, the military, universities, churches, or from the typical "how-to" seminars. It is not the "nuts and bolts" within most organizations that is the problem. Rather, simply stated, the problem is the *quality of their leadership.*

Those who are chosen to lead must be thoroughly grounded in the principles of leadership found in the Holy Word of God. If leadership is built on this "solid ground," the majority of the followers can become heroes and their organizations will achieve success. Hopefully, this realization, followed by the application of the *40 Timeless Principles of Leadership* taken from God's Holy Word, will enable both the aspiring and the experienced leader to continue on a path toward becoming more effective and successful leaders.

As Joshua asked the people of Israel to make a choice (Joshua 24:15), I challenge you to decide today what you will do. Either lead, with God as the center of your leadership; follow another godly leader; or get out of the way so that someone else may lead.

The leadership choice remains yours alone.

END NOTES

1. This concept was created by Harry W. Stephenson, Jr., as part of his doctoral dissertation. The University of Texas, 1963.
2. Colonel Charles F. Austin, *Management's Self-Inflicted Wounds* (New York: Holt, Rinehart and Winston, Inc., 1966), p. 16.
3. *Ibid.*, p. 17.
4. Alan Axelrod, *Patton on Leadership* (Paramus, New Jersey: Prentice Hall Press, 1999), p. 201.
5. This was taken from a story which appeared in the *San Antonio Express News* (Metro Edition), December 20, 2003, p. 1.
6. Patricia A. Pingry, Ed., *The Ideals Treasury of Faith in America* (Nashville: Ideals Publications, a Division of Guideposts, 2003), p. 108.
7. James S. Hewett, Ed., *Illustrations Unlimited* (Wheaton, Illinois: Tyndale, 1988), p. 347.
8. Gene Griessman, *The Words Lincoln Lived By* (New York: Fireside, 1997), p. 19.
9. As printed in Dear Abby, (San Antonio: *San Antonio Express News*, April 11, 1994).
10. *Op. Cit.* Griessman, *The Words Lincoln Lived By*, p. 73.
11. *Ibid.*
12. *The International Dictionary of Thoughts* (Chicago: J. G. Ferguson Publishing Co., 1969), p. 152.
13. *Ibid.*, p. 418.
14. Op. Cit., Griessman, *The Words Lincoln Lived By*, p. 24.
15. *Ibid.*, pp. 36-37.
16. Diane Ravitch, Ed., *The American Reader* (New York: Harper

Collins, 1990), pp. 333-334.

17. George R. Terry, *Principles of Management* (Homewood, Illinois: Richard D. Irwin, Inc., Fifth Edition, 1968), p. 458.
18. William H. Gates, *The Road Ahead* (New York: Viking, 1995), p. 4.
19. Norman L. Frigon, Sr. and Harry K. Jackson, Jr., *The Leader: Developing The Skills & Personal Qualities You Need to Lead Effectively* (New York: American Management Association, 1996), p. 55.
20. Rick Warren, *The Purpose Driven Church: Growth Without Compromising Your Message & Mission* (Grand Rapids, Michigan: Zondervan, 1995), pp. 28; 42.
21. *God's Little Devotional Book for Leaders* (Tulsa: Honor Books, 1997), pp. 20-21.
22. *Op. Cit.*, Axelrod, *Patton on Leadership*, p. 79.
23. *Op. Cit.*, Griessman, *The Words Lincoln Lived By*, p. 20.
24. *Op. Cit.*, Axelrod, *Patton on Leadership*, p. 156.
25. *Op. Cit.*, Frigon and Jackson, *The Leader*, p. 61.
26. *One Hundred and One Famous Poems, An Anthology Compiled by Roy Clark* (Chicago: Contemporary Books, 1958), p. 108.
27. *Op. Cit.*, Griessman, *Words Lincoln Lived By*, p. 104.
28. *Op. Cit.*, *God's Little Devotional Book for Leaders*, p. 267.
29. James O'Toole, *Leadership A to Z: A Guide for the Appropriately Ambitious* (San Francisco: Jossey-Bass Publishers, 1999), p. 168.
30. *Ibid.*, p. 168.
31. *Op. Cit.*, *The International Dictionary of Thoughts*, p. 432.
32. *Op. Cit.*, O'Toole, *Leadership A to Z*, p. 172.
33. *Op. Cit.*, Axelrod, *Patton on Leadership*, p. 155.
34. *Ibid.*
35. *Ibid.*, p. 131.
36. Some of the material presented in this chapter was adapted from a radio broadcast by Dr. David Jeremiah, on *Turning Point*.
37. William J. Federer, *America's God and Country Encyclopedia of Quotations* (Coppell, Texas: FAME Publishing, Inc., 1994), p. 328.

38. Ronald Kessler, *A Matter of Character* (New York: Penguin Group, 2004), pp. 11-12.
39. *Op. Cit.*, Federer, *America's God and Country Encyclopedia of Quotations*, p. 490.
40. *Op. Cit.*, Kessler, *A Matter of Character*, p. 89.
41. *Op. Cit.*, Federer, *America's God and Country Encyclopedia of Quotations*, p. 327.

ABOUT THE AUTHOR

⋆⇥⚬⚬⇤⋆

R. L. Bramble has served as an educator, business executive, motivational speaker, and writer. He holds advanced degrees in business administration (MSBA, DBA) and law (JD). He is a recipient of the honorary degree of Doctor of Sacred Literature. He has held leadership positions in both profit and non-profit organizations and has served as a management consultant and trainer to numerous organizations. He is active in the United Methodist Church where he is a Certified Lay Speaker, an adult church-school teacher, Bible teacher, and a frequent pulpit speaker.

As a student of organizations and leadership, Dr. Bramble has observed various styles of leadership along with those qualities which set the successful leader apart from others. In this book, he has examined the leadership principles as exemplified by various leaders as they are recorded in the Holy Scriptures, both Old and New Testaments. Thus, the title, *Leadership Lessons from the Bible*.

He resides in San Antonio, Texas, with his wife, Kathryn, and is a member of Aldersgate United Methodist Church.

Services Available

Dr. R. L. Bramble is available as a consultant, motivational speaker, or seminar leader to either faith-based or secular organizations that would seek to apply the leadership principles presented in this book.

Also, for information regarding the companion study guide, *Practicing Leadership*, please write or e-mail Dr. Bramble as follows:

P. O. Box 791104
San Antonio, Texas 78279
E-Mail: rlbramble@aol.com

Printed in the United States
47471LVS00003B/139